WHEN WAR IS UNJUST

Being Honest in Just-War Thinking

JOHN HOWARD YODER

Introduction by CHARLES P. LUTZ

AUGSBURG Publishing House • Minneapolis

In gratitude for the witness of:

Martin of Tours, soldier who refused to fight,
  bishop who condemned the capital punishment of heretics;
Martin Luther, theologian who called soldiers to refuse to
  serve in unjust wars;
Martin de Porres, O.P. of Lima, "Father of the poor";
Martin Niemöller, spokesman of the "Confessing Church" in
  resistance to Nazification;
Martin Luther King Jr., who demonstrated that civil disobedi-
  ence is a positive social action;
My sisters and brothers of the Order of St. Martin.

WHEN WAR IS UNJUST
Being Honest in Just-War Thinking

Copyright © 1984 Augsburg Publishing House

Library of Congress Cataloging in Publication Data

Yoder, John Howard.
  WHEN WAR IS UNJUST

  Bibliography: p. 94
  1. Just war doctrine.   2. War—Religious aspects—Mennonite authors.
I. Title.
U21.2.Y63   1984   261.8'73   84-2859
ISBN 0-8066-2077-3

Manufactured in the U.S.A.   APH 10-7084

  2   3   4   5   6   7   8   9   0   1   2   3   4   5   6   7   8   9

Contents

Introduction

John Howard Yoder has done a good deed for all of us who are part of the just-war tradition. The essence of his contribution is a simple challenge. As one who stands outside that tradition (but knows it as well as its best inside theorists), Yoder is saying: *If you want me to take you seriously, show me that you take your tradition seriously.*

And it is certainly beyond doubt that those communities which subscribe to the just-war ethic have done little to (a) teach it to their people, (b) apply it in public policy discussions, and (c) follow its leading when it leads to a conflict with political authority.

So the first point I make in this introduction is one of gratitude to Dr. Yoder, for helping us to see afresh the implications of the just-war tradition and for challenging us who claim it to live in it more faithfully.

Our record of neglect

In my own religious tradition, during my lifetime, the record on the teaching of peace/war ethics has been spotty. During the past 50 years U.S. Lutherans have been through peaks and valleys of concern for restraint in the use of armed force.

During the 1930s, we had a few who were attracted to the worldwide pacifist movement. The Lutheran Peace

Fellowship was formed then, along with numerous other such independent associations within denominations.

With the coming of World War II, however, there was little debate about either pacifism or just/unjust-war ethics, since the need to stop German and Japanese aggression seemed entirely justifiable to most Lutherans. The few who resisted military participation during that war suffered a lonely existence within the Lutheran community.

It is hard to find evidence of serious Lutheran attention to the nuclear weapons debates of the 1950s—in resources for parish education, in the statements of Lutheran church bodies, or in the teaching of the denomination's colleges and seminaries.

A concern for peace/war ethics bloomed among us during the late 1960s and early 1970s, as it did in U.S. society overall, because of the nature of the war in Southeast Asia. Official Lutheran policy statements addressed the morality of the war on the basis of the traditional just/unjust-war theory, and support for selective conscientious objection was first articulated by all major Lutheran church bodies between 1968 and 1970.

Toward the end of the Vietnam War, a major study of the ethics of war and peace in the context of U.S. Lutheranism, *The Witness of U.S. Lutherans on Peace, War, and Conscience,* was produced through the Division of Theological Studies of the Lutheran Council in the U.S.A. On the basis of that document, curriculum for youth and adults on these issues was developed by the church bodies. From 1971 through 1973 the Lutheran Council in the U.S.A. also maintained an office to provide guidance to parishes on the draft law in relation to Lutheran ethical understanding.

After the close of the Vietnam War and the ending of the draft, Lutheran interest in peace/war ethics again waned. It did not revive until the early 1980s, with their growing focus on nuclear weapons escalation.

It is on that peak of interest that we stand as this book appears. We have not learned how to sustain a concern for our ethical tradition on war and peace during the times between global crises. We have yet to commit ourselves to consistent peace education among our children, youth, and adults at all times and places in the church's nurturing ministry.

There are two other points I wish to develop in this introduction: (1) the necessity of some moral framework, in addition to pacifism, for dealing with the reality of lethal force; (2) the dilemma of conflict with government to which the just/unjust-war tradition leads.

The need for a morality of war

It has become popular in recent decades—especially since the development of atomic and thermonuclear weaponry—for some people to say, "The just-war ethic has outlived its usefulness. In an age of mass-destruction weaponry, the just-war criteria no longer apply."

It has always seemed to me that such statements miss the whole point of the just-war tradition, which is, precisely, that *because* warfare is terribly destructive and is inclined to escalate into total devastation there must be a system of restraints, of limits. It is the just-war criteria themselves that, for many nonpacifists today, furnish the tests by which nuclear weapons—and chemical and biological weapons—are declared morally unacceptable.

I believe that any culture which does not adopt the pacifist ethic—and no culture as a whole in today's world has done so—must develop some guidelines restraining the use of force. The alternative is to put into the saddle force itself or those who have most convenient access to force.

An analogy would be that of the police function within our communities. Because of an evident need to protect the innocent and to thwart the destructive impulses of a few, we legitimate the use of force by police officers. We arm them with lethal weapons. We justify their use of such weapons under certain circumstances.

But we do *not* authorize police to use the force at their disposal indiscriminately, arbitrarily, or wantonly. There are rules by which the police must abide. And those rules bear a certain resemblance to the rules of the just-war ethic: use of force must be directed to a specific, limited objective; force must be used in a way that safeguards the innocent; the amount of force must be proportionate to the end sought (don't shoot to kill if you can immobilize); vindictiveness is not permissible; and so on.

The practical alternative to an ethic for restraining the use of lethal force—in domestic police work or in international relations—is not pacifism; it is, rather, unrestrained use of lethal force.

It is exactly at this point that I appreciate the insight of Yoder that the pacifist and just-war traditions "agree most of the time against the other two" positions—the crusade and national-interest wars, neither of which has much room for moral restraint. Before leaving the discussion of the need for a moral framework relating to war, I will suggest three additional reasons why the just-war tradition is useful.

1. The just-war tradition continues to be the ethical bedrock for a significant body of international law on the conduct of warfare, for national military manuals on the same subject, and even for the threat of prosecution for war crimes. That is not a small contribution. At least a partial restraint on the destructiveness of war has resulted. *Some* noncombatants have been protected thereby. *Some* forms of weaponry have been declared illegitimate. And *some* military commanders have been deflected from using disproportionate force.

2. The tradition will be the grounds on which most people who reject nuclear war will do so, whether they know it or not. They will do it on the basis of simple human rationality, weighing factors which are part of the just-war criteria: the need to limit warfare, the need to protect the innocent (noncombatants or civilians, at the very least children and the elderly). Providing people faced by nuclear weapons with a logical, systematic ethic such as the just-war tradition can be quite a help to the reflection process.

3. The tradition offers the ethical guidance by which communities of conscience have been helped to make judgments about their participation in or objection to particular military endeavors. Without something like the just-war tradition, nonpacifists would be adrift with no ethical markers.

Without the just-war tradition, we would immediately set ourselves to inventing something very much like it.

Nothing I have said should be read as a denial that the tradition has obvious weaknesses: it has seldom worked to prevent a war (at least, national leaders are not in the habit of announcing to the world that a war they contemplate is not justifiable and thus will be abandoned); it assumes fairly complete knowledge of the military and political realities on both sides of a conflict; it is designed for a traditional limited-war situation, where combatants can be cleanly separated from populations as a whole. John Howard Yoder speaks at length concerning these weaknesses, and more.

There is, I believe, one additional problem with the ethic of the just war. That is the very name it has carried down through the centuries: "just war." The implication is that a given war can—objectively and theoretically—be *just*. This suggests that a war, or war in general, may be viewed as a positive good.

A better term for the tradition would be "war as lesser evil under well-defined circumstances"—but it is clear why such a label never caught on. I normally prefer to speak of a "just/unjust-war ethic" or a "justifiable-war tradition."

No matter what we call it, there will be an abuse of the ethic in the popular mind. The loyal citizen, especially one familiar with our predominant religious traditions, is likely to argue, "Our churches teach a just-war ethic.

Our government tells me this is a just war. Therefore, I am obligated to support it." The setting and the tools for rigorously testing whether the proposed war (or war in progress) *is* justifiable—for challenging the government's claim—these are simply not available to most Americans. Beginnings have been made in applying the tradition's criteria to public-policy debates during the Vietnam War and the current discussion of U.S. nuclear-weapons policy, and for that we should be grateful.

But if the logic of the justifiable-war ethic is to be followed, then the matter of disagreeing with one's political leadership continues to be an important issue. And that brings us to the second major introductory consideration.

The disobedience dilemma

Dr. Yoder suggests that, in practice, most citizens in nations of the West (those most influenced by the assumptions of the just-war tradition) have followed throughout the centuries and at the present moment continue to follow neither pacifism nor an ethic of justifiable war. In fact, most of us have adhered to a crusader ("this is God's holy war") or a national-interest ("my nation, right or wrong") ethic. I believe he is correct.

One reason it is difficult for us to give more than lip service to our supposedly "orthodox" ethic of war is that the just-war tradition inevitably leads to the real possibility of conflict with the law.[1]

We can examine the dilemma by imagining a functioning draft in the midst of some U.S. military enterprise that lacks broad popular support, such as a plan to send combat troops into the oil region of the Persian Gulf or into Central America. Let us suppose that Congress has voted to renew the draft and is inducting large numbers of young American males. Most of them prefer, for reasons of personal convenience, not to be conscripted into armed service. A substantial number, in addition, have learned something of the criteria for justifiable use of armed force as children and youth in their churches and in family discussions. They sincerely believe that their nation's proposed use of their persons in the present context is not justifiable according to the criteria.

Pacifist friends of these young people would have no major problem with the government, since objection to participation in all wars is recognized under the draft law. Pacifists must still demonstrate to the draft system that they are sincere, and they will still have to serve in noncombatant roles (either in the military or as civilians) if called. But there is no philosophical reason for conflict between them and the government.

The particular-war objector, however, would have a serious problem under such circumstances. The law does not recognize the right of a citizen to make judgments about the morality of *specific* wars or military enterprises and then to withhold service as a combatant on the basis of such judgments. The irony is that a position held by relatively few of our citizens ("all wars are immoral") is recognized under our draft law as valid; the view supposedly emanating from the religious tradition claimed by the great majority of Americans ("each war must be judged by strict ethical criteria") has no legal status under the draft law.

From a practical governmental perspective it is understandable why all-war objectors are excused from service in combat and selective objectors are denied that right. It would be immensely difficult to determine fairly who qualifies and who does not for selective objection—to say nothing of the far larger numbers who could be expected to seek such status.

But there is a profoundly political reason as well why the position of selective participation/objection has found little support among lawmakers. Pacifists are not, in the end, questioning their own government's policy in undertaking a specific military activity. It is war *itself*, by any nation at any time in history, that is the object of their rejection. Their own ability to participate through the bearing of arms is equally impossible no matter whose war it is or what the cause. Selective objectors, however, are necessarily at odds with a *specific* military policy of their government at a specific time. And that is quite a different matter for the government to address than the perhaps inconvenient but relatively innocuous problem of excusing from combat the few who can persuasively claim a totally pacifist world view.

Ethically speaking, it is rather troubling that we are in such a situation. I would argue that selective participants/objectors who come to a particular military enterprise with careful, conscientious judgments about its morality and then refuse participation on the basis of such moral reasoning are engaging more consciously in moral conduct than are total pacifists. In adopting the position that they can never, under any circumstances, engage in bearing arms, principled pacifists have put the decision *beyond* the realm of moral judgments conditioned by day-to-day circumstances.

Those who seek to follow an ethic such as the just/unjust-war tradition rather than one of universal principle ("all use of armed force is always wrong") are left without a legal place to stand. It is because of this dilemma that the religious communities following a justifiable-war ethic must be very clear: those who run afoul of their own nation's laws because they follow that ethic deserve the fullest support of their churches. To be consistent, those churches ought to advocate change in the conscription law so that selective participation/objection regarding combat service is made legal. But until and unless the law is changed, those churches must stand with their young people who find themselves in civil disobedience out of faithfulness to the ethic they have learned.

This dilemma also should remind us that what is legal and what is moral are not always the same. Law and ethics each have their own logic. Sometimes they will be in conflict.

Conclusion

Some additional observations from the perspective of a Lutheran "justifiable-war" ethicist may be useful.

1. Yoder points out that the tradition of the just war is not dogma for Roman Catholics, but has been given confessional status by Lutherans and other Reformation churches. True, the Lutherans' Augsburg Confession (Article 16) mentions participation in a just war as one of the activities in which Christians may engage. But the point of Article 16 is something else: that Lutherans understand God to be active through the structures of the civil order to bring about justice and peace, and that believers are expected to take part in those structures, such as family and government. Serving as soldiers "in a just war" is but one illustration, along with paying taxes and marrying. Thus it seems to me that no argument can be made that all Lutherans are bound to adopt the just-war position as their ethic on peace and war. Lutherans are free to opt for pacifism or some other ethic, without thereby diminishing their credentials within the Lutheran family. In other words, adherence to the just-war ethic is not a characteristic mark of Lutheran confessionalism in the way that the doctrine of justification by grace or the emphasis on a theology of the cross are commonly understood to be. (I think the same freedom concerning ethics of peace and war is available to Anglicans, Calvinists, and others whose 16th-century creeds may mention the just-war tradition.)

2. It is sometimes suggested that people who follow the just/unjust-war approach are likely to be war-oriented or war-accepting. There is clear evidence that genuine adherents to the tradition are resigned to the reality of war in our world and are eager to do something about both the quantity and the quality of the use of armed force among nations. But that is not at all the same as to say that just-war theorists are responsible for leading national leaders and peoples into an acceptance of war.

As Gary J. Quinn has said, "Proper understanding of just-war theory will no more make one a warmonger than proper understanding of pacifism will turn one into a coward." [2]

3. The essential origin of anything like the just-war ethic, in terms of the biblical faith, is the overarching concern of love for one's neighbor. I understand pacifists to begin there also, leading to the argument that violence is never a way to show love to a neighbor, including a neighbor who is my enemy. But I see just-war ethics as being equally concerned with such love. The difference is that another set of neighbors receives primary attention: those who may be called the innocent, those who are in need of protection from attack, those who would be defenseless unless someone took up arms on their behalf. It is finally that question, "How shall the defenseless neighbor be protected?" which just-war theory is seeking to address. Any other question (such as, "How shall my nation remain supreme in the world?" or "How can the comfortable life-style we have be maintained?") is not a legitimate one for the just-war ethic.

4. The justifiable-war ethic is an ethic for war avoidance or war restraint. It is *not* a set of criteria for building a just peace, that is, a world of peace with justice. I have suggested elsewhere (Chapter 11 in *Peaceways* [Augsburg, 1983]) that the churches are called to greater seriousness about constructing a "just-security ethic." While that is a different task than the present book can encompass, the need is obvious. It is also one to which both pacifists and followers of the just-war tradition are drawn if they are serious about ending the violence of war, since ultimately war can be eliminated only through the establishment of conditions which nurture justice, security, and freedom.

5. John Howard Yoder, a pacifist thinker of international renown, is honoring those who stand in the just-

war tradition by the pages which follow. He speaks to us as close kin. He is not setting out to denigrate or demolish the just-war ethic. Rather, he is calling us to integrity within the framework of our own claims. He asks us, for the sake of the world, to demonstrate the credibility of our ethic, to put it to the test, to be honest about where it leads us. He remains skeptical, but he is also open to being shown that the just-war ethic *can* make a difference in our time. I am grateful to him for the gift he offers us.

Charles P. Lutz, Director
Office of Church in Society
The American Lutheran Church

Preface

Ecumenical encounter is defined by the recognition that if we differ about conclusions, we probably differ about the kinds of logic and the historical paths whereby we got to those contradictory conclusions. Respectful dialog therefore demands the exercise of entering into the interlocutor's stance and story, if one wishes to locate any common court of appeal, before which to adjudicate the contradictory claims of two (or more) holistically opposed positions.

Precisely because of its age-old numerical domination and its commonsensical quality, the "justifiable-war" tradition articulated by most Christian thinkers for a millennium and a half is especially in need of such benefit-of-the-doubt explication. Most people who hold to that view have not thought about it much. Some (to whom Charles Lutz refers in his introduction) are in fact applying it when they say that they reject it. Others, who say they hold to it, do not in fact so reason or act. It would then be misleading to seek to debate with that tradition, as if its meaning were clear and univocal, before helping it to define itself in such a way as to stand up to evaluation. It is to that clarification that the present text seeks to contribute.

The study behind this book was supported by the faculty-improvement program of the University of Notre Dame with assistance from the Carnegie Mellon Foundation, and by Goshen Biblical Seminary, with aid from the deFehr Foundation. Lectures similar to this text but briefer have been presented to the University of New Mexico, Harvard Divinity School, Gordon Conwell Divinity School, New College for Advanced Christian Studies at Berkeley, Regent College, and Calvin College.

1

The Quest to
Make War Moral

The dominant view of Christians since the early Middle
Ages concerning the morality of war is officially supposed to be the "just-war tradition" (JWT). Affirmed
implicitly by Ambrose (d. 397) and Augustine (d. 430),
integrated into the system of Christian moral thought by
Thomas Aquinas, unfolded in a system of its own by
Francisco de Vitoria (d. 1546) and Francisco Suarez (d.
1617), this teaching appears in all of the encyclopedias
and manuals as what most Christians are supposed to
believe. It is explicitly affirmed in the official documents
of Lutherans, Anglicans, and Presbyterians.

To define it simply: as distinguished from amoral,
"realistic," or "national-interest" approaches which say
one cannot think morally about war, from the "crusad-
ing" approach which sees war as a holy cause, and from
pacifism which rejects war in principle, the just-war
tradition considers war an evil but claims that under
specific circumstances it is justifiable as less evil than
the execution of some threat which it wards off or the
continuation of some system which it changes.

It is appropriate to speak rather of a "tradition" than
of a "doctrine" or a "theory," for there is no one official
statement of this approach to which all would subscribe.
Its essence is the recognition of a set of criteria calculated to measure with some clarity and objectivity when

it may be held to be the case that the evil of war is justifiable because the other evil which it prevents is greater.

Later we shall need to look more carefully at these criteria. At the beginning of our description it suffices to list the most obvious ones in the simplest formulation.

The simplest criteria

1. The authority waging the war must be legitimate.
2. The cause being fought for must be just.
3. The ultimate goal ("intention") must be peace.
4. The subjective motivation ("intention") must not be hatred or vengefulness.
5. War must be the last resort.
6. Success must be probable.
7. The means used must be indispensable to achieve the end.
8. The means used must be discriminating, both
   (a) quantitatively, in order not to do more harm than the harm they prevent ("proportionality"), and
   (b) qualitatively, to avoid use against the innocent ("immunity").
9. The means used must respect the provisions of international law.

A glance at the parallel literature shows that this particular listing is only one of many formulations.[1] Often they are grouped in two categories, one governing the choice to go to war, *jus ad bellum* (1-6 above), and the others governing proper conduct in the midst of hostilities, *jus in bello*. The variety of listings and ways in which the criteria are formulated is itself a problem, if one is asking that the tradition be precise; but to work at interpreting the varieties of definition, to say nothing of resolving the differences, would go far beyond our present assignment.

This is the position which most Christians, if asked, would say they hold to, which most bishops, pastors, and theologians would exposit. But is that really true? Do they really believe it? And if people who really believe it really apply it, how does that look? As a contribution to the integrity and self-esteem of people in those mainstream communities, the present study examines the credibility of that dominant tradition.

Can it be made credible?

What do we mean when we ask of a theory or of a system of thought that it be credible? The just-war tradition (JWT) presents itself as an instrument for making decisions, for discernment in the face of a variety of possible interpretations of the morality of violence. The tradition comprises a set of criteria which appear to be applicable to specific data in a political and military conflict. They would seem, on first sight, to include some and to exclude other expressions of military violence to which people in that situation would normally contemplate recourse. That such weapons and strategies might be used —i.e., that the criteria might function to permit war— does not need to be demonstrated. What needs therefore to be tested is whether the criteria can really function so as in any specific cases to *exclude* a particular cause, a particular weapon, a particular strategy, a particular tactical move.

This question of credibility divides naturally into four sets of questions, of which the first will occupy us the most lengthily:

1. There is the question of the *conceptual* adequacy of the tradition. Are concepts and terms defined in such a way that effective application can reliably follow when the generally stated criteria encounter real cases?

2. What are the *social* prerequisites for the criteria to operate? What kind of institutional form and what decision-making instruments would be demanded?

3. What are the *psychological* requisites? What kinds of people are ready to make moral judgments independently of the authorities? How do we produce such people?

4. What would be the *moral* requirements? In at least most cases in which a negative judgment on a particular war or particular military action would be called for by the honest application of the JWT, this honest and negative judgment will involve some risk or some sure sacrifice. What are the moral prerequisites for individuals and groups to be willing to run those risks or consent to those sacrifices?

In traditional debate between proponents of the JWT and the advocates of other Christian views, the challenges have been most often of two kinds:
1. Has there ever been a just war that would meet all the requirements? It is a worthy test of a tool of moral discourse to ask whether it can ever wholly apply. Yet its friends can continue to claim that it has some value even if the requirements are never perfectly met. The requirements of other moral visions usually fall short of complete satisfaction. The teaching might then be held to be meaningful without ever producing a perfect case.
2. Has anyone ever said no, in a situation of great military or political pressure, to an action which would be against the rules?
These foreshortened and popularized ways of putting the question are not morally illegitimate, but they will do us less good than the fuller way I propose here to put the challenge of being honest in just-war thinking.

Why should a critic care?

Why would it be worthwhile, from the perspective of my pacifist commitment, to favor the development of a credible just-war tradition?
1. It would first of all serve to affirm the integrity of my interlocutors, those fellow Christians or fellow humans who claim that they are neither idolators sacrificing their fellow creatures to the absolute value of national interest nor murderers killing without any discipline nor crusaders, but that they limit the violence for which they will

soberly accept responsibility to the necessary minimum evil. I must be committed, on general "ecumenical" grounds, to giving the benefit of the doubt to people who make that claim. But my taking them seriously demands that I ask of them that they make their claim operational, rather than stating it as a cover which they do not intend to live up to.

2. Even though the moral logic with which we argue is different in general and contradictory at some points, every time a just-war thinker exercises effective *discipline,* the relative effect thereof will be parallel to my concerns; it will save human lives and other values that would have been destroyed if there had not been that restraint.

3. On the level of conceptual clarification, it will be a great gain to have overcome the three popular platitudes with which discussion in this area has been hobbled:

a. *That the just-war tradition is the majority view by which most Christians involved in political responsibility have been living.* We shall see that effective adherence to the limitations implicit in the just-war tradition is a rarity: that at many points people who *say* they hold to such views have not begun to develop the tools to make them stick; and that most of the time most people, without avowing it, are fighting national-interest wars or holy wars.

b. *That the basic ethical issue is to choose between the just-war tradition and the pacifist tradition.* We shall see that these two positions agree most of the time against the other two, and that in most contemporary situations of real moral choice, whether in the face of the ideological "war of liberation" or of the world-threatening nuclear exchange, the two views would have the same impact.

c. *That acceptance of the just-war view is generally, if not universally, compatible with involvement in responsible political office.* The people who put "just war" in the Protestant creeds rejected pacifism because they thought it amounted to withdrawal from responsibility. Yet just-war criteria are pointless if they cannot also demand, situationally, the refusal of some acts apparently commanded by the national interest. In modern times the person holding honestly to a just-war position may well be obliged to withdraw at least from certain military responsibilities (what has recently come to be called "selective conscientious objection") and certain high levels of civilian command, if that command involvement is seen as taking moral responsibility for what actually goes on in the war.

But before leaping to the question of credibility itself we need a broader acquaintance with what the tradition is about. It is not only a set of criteria which ask questions of authority, cause, intention, means. It is as well a long history of thought and application, with more twists and turns along the way than are normally dealt with when the tradition's application is being discussed. Some of our contemporaries take JWT as a piece of modern government theory without reference to earlier origins. Some Christians, on the other hand, claim that it is a correct position because it was expressed by early medieval Catholic theologians, and give no attention to what has happened to the tradition since then.

For our purposes, even though this account must be unavoidably superficial, it is important to study how the tradition evolved before we ask about its present viability. The history here recounted being rather well-established, little annotation will be needed.[2]

2

The Just-War Tradition in Its Medieval Context

Few citizens participate

The participation in regrettable but unavoidable violence that was authorized by the medieval tradition was not permitted to most people. This authorization was given to the prince, whose status was tested by the criterion of legitimate authority, and to those under his command. For institutional and economic reasons his soldiers were few: a small number of knights whose vocational definition included the honor with which they insisted on fighting fair, and a larger but fluctuating number of mercenaries. The authorization of both groups to fight was derived morally from the prince's own authority as prince. They had no patriotic stake in the war aims. The mercenaries had no personal moral preference as to which side should win except for the salary, privileges of plunder, the desire for a good fight, and the desire to stay alive. The knights had high moral principles, but the nation was not the object of their loyalty. Ordinary citizens, including the able-bodied adult males, were thought of as not apt for military service. They needed to stay with their farming or their trades in order to bring in the tax money to pay for the war. There were specific moral theories to interpret why most people should not be categorized with the knights and mercenaries as having a right (to say nothing of any duty) to participate in war.

Only at the very edge of medieval theory were there exceptions to the above, as in the case where, in an emergency, militia duty might be permitted for local self-defense. But such an exception could arise only in time of immediate threat, not as a basis of military strategy on a larger-than-local scale.

The common people, who did not constitute a part of the military class, having no skills and no weapons, were exempt from military service. Other classes of people as well were exempt from any obligation to serve, even in local self-defense. This included all the religious and the secular clergy, with the very special exception of the military monks (the Teutonic Knights, the knights of the orders of Malta and of Jerusalem). It applied as well to pilgrims and penitents, i.e., persons (even lay persons) under a specific spiritual discipline for the purpose of special spiritual renewal or purging the guilt of past sins. Thus the people allowed to fight in a just war were but a small minority of the population.

God's peace, God's truce

The major impact of the church as institution on war as an institution was not in its moral teaching about the just war, but rather in the framework of other social-hygiene measures, taken often by local bishops and sometimes by higher authorities (synods, popes).

1. The "Peace of God" was such a measure. It was a formally recognized way of proclaiming that a particular spiritual status attaches to certain places, so that there must be no fighting there, or to certain persons, so that there must be no violence involving them.

2. The "Truce of God" was another such measure: a specific proclamation by an ecclesiastical authority, the moral validity of which did not depend upon the agreement of the combatant parties, providing that during certain periods there should be no battle (none on Sun-

days, holy days, during Lent, etc.). Since the supply and transportation, rest and recreation needs of medieval soldiers were enormous, it is not really sure whether limiting formal hostilities to certain days of the week or year, or to certain places, decreased the carnage proportionately, as long as both sides complied. But at least it made two points visible in the awareness of common people: that the church wanted to limit war, and that all Christian people were to accept those limitations and make it a point of integrity to fight fair within them.

Beyond the "Peace of God" and the "Truce of God" there was also in certain periods a very aggressive mediatorial effort of bishops (when they were not themselves the combatant princes). They intervened as peacemakers between neighboring princes in order to reduce the destruction.

The social context in which the just-war tradition was cultivated was not primarily that of a prince or his advisor looking objectively at a military project ahead of time and deciding on its advisability in terms of national or dynastic interests and its legitimacy in terms of just-war criteria. The patterns of public decision making before democratic times did not include that kind of upfront openness about how decisions are made and why. The social context of the just-war tradition was rather in the realm of the confessional and canon law. The criteria became operative when the question arose as to whether a knight returning from battle could be permitted to receive the Eucharist, and what difference it made in that connection whether the war was just or not.

Even for killing in a *just* cause some period of penance was demanded. Even for killing in a *just* cause a candidate for the priesthood could be rendered incapable of receiving orders. These judgments applied even to a person whose participation in killing was no more than serving on a jury that condemned someone to the death penalty.

The difference in form and type of penance called for was the point at which just-war details were worked out the most thoroughly, so that our most informative recent scholarly source on just-war thought in the Middle Ages is based largely on canon law.[1]

Under the category of "just cause" the earlier fathers had included two distinct kinds of warrant: (1) properly political matters, such as the occupation of territory or unpaid debts, and (2) more directly religious matters like blasphemy or a divine command. These two kinds of warrant call for two kinds of reasoning. By the end of the Middle Ages they had begun to be disentangled. The concept *just war* was still used to cover them both, meaning in the broadest sense that military action was morally permissible, but two different sets of moral arguments were developing, with the "crusade" becoming distinguishable from the "properly political" just war.

Holy war vs. just war

Crusade is a Christian term. If we were to speak in more general terms we should use *holy war*. This was present as well in early Israel, in Islam, and in other religious cultures. For contemporary purposes we might expand it even further to recognize post-Enlightenment "ideological wars" as having the same moral structure.

The holy war differs from the "just war" (I shall henceforth use the latter term in its narrower, later, "properly political" sense) in five ways:

1. *Its cause has a transcendent validation.* What is at stake is not a finite political value needing to be weighed over against other political values, so that proportionality and the clash of rights and interests of various parties in the social mechanism need to be calculated carefully. The warriors are freed from such properly political calculations by the overarching value of the holy cause.

2. *This transcendent quality is known by revelation:* the measurement does not arise simply and empirically out of a sober measurement of a situation. It must be brought to us from beyond the picture we ourselves have of the predicament.

This information from beyond the system normally will need to be communicated by a special kind of person or institution that can bring such information: by a prophet or an oracle. In churches with a strong institutional frame, the validation will need to be pronounced by a pope, a bishop, or a council. In other religions or in modern ideologies this same function is discharged by an ideological oracle like an Ayatollah, a Chairman Mao, or a Central Committee.

3. *The adversary has no rights,* or at least no vested rights that demand calculation in firm, proportional ways. Sometimes, as in the Iberian invasion of South America, this logic was visible in the debates about whether the natives had souls. Usually it is associated with racist or ethnic deprecation or depreciation of the enemy: the only good enemy is a dead enemy. Restraint is no virtue. Excess may be a sign of devotion.

4. *The criterion of last resort does not apply.* Other ways of achieving the same goal — accepting half a loaf as better than nothing, mediation, and compromise — are dishonorable in the face of the transcendent duty.

5. *It need not be winnable.* To fail in a holy cause is a moral victory. In the medieval period, for both Muslim and Christian, to die in a holy war was the surest and quickest path to heaven. Even in the modern analogs there is a kind of immortality assigned to martyrs, which, as Latin Americans can testify, is seen in the special status of Che Guevara or Sandino.

Once the concept of holy war has been defined with some clarity, it drops out of our study. The Roman Catholic hierarchy has proclaimed no crusade since the late Middle Ages. The questions raised by thinking that there can be such a war are quite different from the ones we shall be pursuing here. Yet historically speaking, it should be noted that when appeal is made to transcendent ideological causes not subject to political measurement, like the defense of "the free world" or the liberation of "the working class," it is in fact the holy-war concept that is still at work.

National self-interest

Toward the end of the medieval period there developed yet another distinguishable line of reasoning. One can argue that it was always intrinsically there, but that it took the Renaissance to bring it to the surface. Machiavelli (d. 1527) is credited with surfacing honestly the claim that the prince is both the only judge and the only validation of value in his nation. Autonomous national interest is the only ultimately meaningful and binding appeal. Moral language might still be used in a subordinate way, as one of the tools of politics, sometimes to get people to keep their promises to you (the prince), and to make them think you are a good person, if that would be helpful; but the obligation to tell the truth or keep one's promises or respect the sanctity of life is never absolute if the ultimate welfare of the ruling house itself can be served by sacrificing those values in particular cases.

When Machiavelli spelled out this autonomy of the prince's power and welfare, it was defended over against three alternative concerns:

1. The rights and concerns of the prince's own people.
2. The rights and concerns of other princes to whom he may have obligations.
3. The rights and concerns of the moral order—if there is such a thing, whether expressed by priests or by philosophers or just present in the nature of things.

The position taken by Machiavelli in politics in general is too broad for us to discuss. We are asking only about the morality of war, not about the rights of citizens. The notion that national interest is an autonomous value, subject to no higher adjudication, is a point independent of some of the autocratic implications of Machiavelli. Modern Western political theory as expressed by the late Hans Morgenthau affirms the autonomous value of national interest in relations between nations, while not denying the accountability of governments to their own people. Certain versions of the doctrine of the divine right of kings used to affirm the total autonomy of moral decisions as residing in the ruler over against the people or over against other nations, yet saw in this not an exemption from a religious moral order but rather a specific mandate given by God to the ruler.

Thus for our purposes what we identify as a third and new type of nonpacifist position is the autonomy of the national interest. Some will also use the phrase *just war* to describe this phenomenon. Negatively, it says war is not wrong. Yet it denies explicitly or implicitly the obligation or the possibility that the military operation might or should be judged in the light of objective criteria. Thereby operationally it rejects just-war reasoning in the precise and proper sense.

Although the bluntness with which Machiavelli had spelled out the principle of open selfishness offended many, not long after his time people who considered themselves morally far more serious accepted the same kind of notion under the heading of "national sovereignty." The end of the feudal networks and of the empire in favor of strong independent nations was accepted by most currents of opinion as a step forward. For Machiavelli it was the prince who needed to take no fundamental account of the rights of others. Now it became the nation as a body, but that autonomy was incarnated especially in the ruling house or government (however chosen and maintained in office). National loyalty was expected to be for all citizens a value above the world solidarity either of humankind or of the faith. The notion of national sovereignty itself, although its effect was usually to make some particular authoritarian government exempt from deep criticism, was still somehow interpreted as a dimension of the dignity and freedom of all the people of the nation. All of this naturally decreased radically the ability of anybody to challenge the moral autonomy of a given government within its own territory.

Thus, since the end of the Middle Ages, there have been

three kinds of nonpacifist logic available, though they were hardly separated in patriotic discourse or day-to-day politics: autonomous national self-interest, holy war, and the justifiable war (whose warrants are authentically political).

Justifiable, yet sinful?

Interpreters are agreed that "justifiable" is a more precise adjective than "just," since no claim is made that the actions involved in a justifiable war are in themselves positively righteous. The mainstream of the tradition does not say that the military actions are morally imperative, but only that a case can be made for them and that someone who finds that he must do them is not to be treated as morally irresponsible. Some adherents would still say that the actions committed in the just war are sinful in some profound sense and constantly stand in need of forgiveness. This is the case especially with those for whom the concept of sin is defined in deeper than ethical ways. Others would reject the word *sinful* but would still talk about the destruction worked by a just war as materially evil, not as good. Thus when in our text we use the habitual and more concise phrase *just war*, it is regularly to be understood as shorthand for the more accurate "justifiable war."

One last observation is imperative if we are to be fair to the Middle Ages. The moral thinkers who developed this body of tradition — both the confessors and canon lawyers measuring the gravity of particular offenses and the systematic writers toward the end of the medieval period—did not see themselves as making a positive case for the politics of establishment, as blessing what was actually being done by their rulers. Most of them were fundamentally sad about the difference between the city of God and the city of man. As Roland Bainton says specifically of Augustine, the concession that such lethal measures could not be avoided is morally valid only when it is "mournful," a concession rather than a mandate, a regrettable dirty duty rather than an intrinsically righteous obedience.

The counterculture perspective was clear from the very beginning when Ambrose could use the justifiable-war tradition (and his own considerable experience as a lay politician before he had become a bishop) as leverage to motivate and articulate a concrete critical focus against injustices committed by his emperor Theodosius. At the other end of the Middle Ages Vitoria did the same as critic of the Iberian adventures in South America. Thus the just-war ethic was the dominant, but not the only, moral guidance given to public life in the Middle Ages by the Roman Catholic Church. Nor was the impact of that tradition an uncritical acceptance of the wars that were then going on.

3

Weakening
the Restraints

The medieval heritage is far from our age. We must survey the path from then to now to observe the growth of the just-war tradition in both its constancy and its flexibility. There will need to be growth and transformation before the just-war ideas become usable as guidance for actual decision making in positions of political responsibility.

Since our interest in this rapid survey of historical development is to sketch the background for contemporary credibility, our summary will be schematic. We turn first of all to those developments between the Middle Ages and the present which have tended to decrease the ability of the JWT to provide restraint.

The Reformation

The first profound and global changes come with the Protestant Reformation. Most Protestants assume that the JWT is one of the points, perhaps one of the few, where Protestants took over the substance of Roman Catholic moral consensus without debate and therefore without change. This is what some Protestant leaders thought at the time, but it was not the whole truth.

The social form of the Protestant Reformation, which

seemed indispensable if the doctrinal renewal promoted by the Reformers was to survive politically, was a church structured by the state. Theologians for the universities and pastors for the parishes were accredited and named —and often paid—by princes and city councils. The ways in which this took place differed considerably in detail, if we contrast the Anglican, Lutheran, and Calvinist systems. But they had in common the conviction that it was not only permissible but theologically correct, even mandatory, that the visible institution called "the church" should be subject to—in fact brought into being by—the administrative authority of the civil government.

Not only in social and psychological realism, but also in theoretical intention, this had the unavoidable effect of decreasing the likelihood that a theologian or a pastor would be a source of critical perspective on decisions being made by princes and politicians — who were at the same time his employers. An exceptionally courageous Zwingli or Calvin or Knox could sometimes bite the hand that fed him, but the institutional arrangements were not such as to foster or provoke that quality of intellectual distance. As a matter of fact, when these men did differ from their political protectors, it was more often in the other direction. That is, Zwingli and Knox were likely to advocate *more* use of violence in both religious and civil matters than the civil authorities thought wise, rather than appealing to JWT categories to restrain their rulers.

The Protestant Reformation escalated the importance of the JWT by giving it creedal status. The major Reformation confessions specifically affirm the doctrine. Some of them link this confirmation with an express condemnation of those who believe otherwise. In the medieval context it would not have occurred to Augustine or Thomas to think of these matters as dogma. They were assumed to be part of the self-evident consensus that everybody already, naturally, knew. It was possible in the Middle Ages, and it is still possible today, for a Roman Catholic Christian to reject the just-war tradition and not be identified as a heretic. There has never been a normative proclamation or promulgation by a synod or a pope, speaking *ex cathedra* or otherwise, to make the acceptance of this doctrine necessary for Catholics. No dogma has stood in the way of the resurgence of pacifism among Roman Catholics in recent decades. On the other hand, the just-war tradition is theoretically obligatory for Protestants of those mainstream traditions where the Reformation was implemented by a government and fixed in a confession.

Perhaps still more weighty in terms of proportion and social impact, the Protestant Reformation took what was previously an exceptional concession made to the sovereign and his employees and made it the norm for all citizens. No longer were clergy, pilgrims, or penitents exempted. Such special persons were thought by the reformers to represent the notion of salvation by works and spiritual privilege which the Reformation had swept away. Special times and places (the "Truce of God" and the "Peace of God") also were no longer operational.

The Protestant Reformation also provided new occasions for righteous violence. The defense of the Reformation itself, the freedom of preaching, and the Protestant status of a reformed province became the objects of military hostilities off and on for the next century. Europe was beginning to break up into sovereign nations; the Reformation accelerated the disintegration and gave it a good conscience. Since it had been determined that the religion of a province should be decided by that of the sovereign, the only means by which the cause of religious truth could be defended, fostered, or even advanced would be military or diplomatic. Therefore Europe was to see a series of wars of religion, bringing into the heartland of Christendom the escalation of religious claims which previously had been reserved for hostilities against the infidel. Just at a time when Catholic tradition had begun to disentangle the no-holds-barred crusade from the civilly justifiable but also restrainable war, intranecine confessional battles restored to Christendom the reality of the crusade without the name. Half of the middle of Europe was destroyed in the name of God.

Not only did the Reformation bring about wars *between* nations on the grounds of confessional hostility, it provided as well the basis for an escalation of the notion of righteous revolution. The idea that there could be a moral justification for not being subject to an unjust regime was already present in the thought of Thomas Aquinas, but only as an intellectual exercise. His way of saying it was that sedition is always immoral, but that in a situation of very bad government it is the bad prince who is guilty of sedition, and the people who revolt against him are therefore not seditious but defenders of good government.

Neither Thomas nor the lawyers of his time had spelled this out in real terms, but the Reformation did. At the end of the 16th century Reformed Christians, responding to the massacre of St. Bartholomew's Night in France (1573) and to the Inquisition in the Low Countries, and Catholics, responding to their expulsion from England, began to develop in a literary way a doctrine of justified revolution. "Tyrannicide" was the simplest form in which it was natural that this doctrine should first develop. This concept presupposed that the source of the evil in a culture was centered in one bad ruler, so that if he were removed, good government could come back to normal, thereby minimizing violence (if successful). Yet the doctrine immediately deepened, with appeals to concepts of political covenant, explaining that the ruler had his authority in the first place because there was a civil covenant between him and his subjects, and that the obligation of subjects to respect him was conditional, being subject to suspension by virtue of his bad performance.

Thus we see the origins of social-contract theory coming first not from the French Enlightenment but from Reformation and Counter-Reformation theories of righteous insurrection. These theories had not yet produced the violence they were capable of, but they had the effect of setting aside in one further way the initial restraining impulse of the JWT. They contributed to the independence of the Netherlands and of Scotland.

Enlightenment

The second broad set of changes tending away from restraint are those we find associated with the Enlightenment, the second major wave of cultural change in Western history of which we must take account.

The value of the nation became secularized, disconnected from religious sanctions and controls. On the one hand, this arose from a degree of disgust with the way religious motivations had led the nations of Europe into destructive and wasteful combat. Now politics was reduced to matters of functional utility rather than crusades. Yet with the same blow the values of the nation became autonomous, withdrawn from the scope of moral criticism by the theologians and the churches. Thus by decreasing the likelihood of a crusade, humanists increased the power of a Machiavelli.

One of the marks of political criticism in this age was the growing importance of the citizen and of the social covenant as a basis for the effort to diminish the authority of rulers. Yet the more we call upon a government to be accountable to its own people, the easier we make it for that government and its own populace to take less account of the world community and of the competing rights of other nations. Campaigns of hatred or suspicion against other nations become one of the ways a government has to gain support from its own people and to divert criticism from its own vices.

The notion of revolution was also secularized. For the revolutionary thinkers of the 16th century, the offense of a king that made him worthy to be unseated had been his failure to permit or protect the true preaching of the gospel or the practice of the faith. Now a regime could be declared unworthy of loyalty on the gounds of criteria drawn from a political philosophy or ideology, matters which are still more difficult to adjudicate with any objectivity. Every political doctrine can accredit some spokesmen to proclaim that any specific regime has forfeited its legitimacy. What began with the criticism of royalty by a few elite philosophers in the 17th century became in the 18th a blank check for almost any political doctrine to call for the violent unseating of almost any regime.

Total war

A third major early modern development is that war has become "total" in a number of different ways, each of them decreasing the possibility of effective restraint. The phenomena which later came to be called "total war" began to arise in the age of revolution, especially in France. Every French citizen was claimed as a supporter of the cause. The revolutionary ideology claims that the restructuring of society is done in the name of all "the people." Then every citizen is a partisan. War is no longer between dynasties or royal houses but between nations as wholes. Since every citizen is a partisan, there is no longer the same evident meaning to the thought that civilians should be treated as noncombatants.

Hand in hand with the change in ideology went a change in the management of the political system: it became possible to mobilize almost everyone. Every citizen is a soldier. Wars are won less by position, which can depend on a decisive battle, and more by attrition, depending on the total strength of the enemy's economy and society. The economy can be directed in such a way that even the civilian economic productivity is increasingly understood to be contributing to the war effort. Everyone is in some sense a combatant, not only in moral commitment to the national cause, but also as part of a unified war economy. No longer is the warrior class a select minority with an elite ethos.

Not only is the entire population economically mobilized; not only are all able-bodied men subject to call to serve as soldiers—the Napoleonic age also made regular what had been a rarity before, a standing army of citizen soldiers. They were drawn from the entire population, or at least from most of its lower social strata, by obligation rather than by lifelong profession. This created a new relationship between the population as a whole and the army and thereby between the population and the government.

Escalation via technologies

These three changes correlate with a fourth: the technology of manufacturing, transportation, weaponry, and communication escalated exponentially the capacity to destroy and the speed with which harm could be done. In the good old days a war involved delays of weeks during which troops would move on foot from one front to another, time during which diplomacy could proceed more rapidly than deployment. Notions of last resort have therefore lost the real meaning they once had, and the quantitative measurements of proportion and discrimination need to be thought of on a completely different scale.

The growth of the idea that the state represents all its people would seem to provide some new leverage for the criticism of military adventure, especially in view of the fact that the victims in war tend to be the sons of the "people," who are called to be soldiers more than the sons of the rulers, who make the choices to go to war. Thus the rhetoric of pacifism has often spoken of war as an activity of aristocrats whom the common people should refuse to support. Yet seldom did that concept effectively portray the popular mentality. Democracy seems rather to have increased the space for demagoguery.

In order to gain a popular mandate, politicians may think they must bid up the nationalistic and xenophobic enthusiasm of common people, thereby putting themselves under pressure to perform in a way as "patriotic" as their campaign language. Thus the medieval vision of the prince as a responsible and wise decision maker, able to lead his people because he knew more of the facts and had learned the craft of governing, was replaced by elected politicians who become prisoners of the patriotic sentiments their campaigning stirred up. Whether we speak of the relatively genuine democracies, in which popular suffrage is effective, or of the many places in which the facade of democracy is used to cover less worthy designs, it often appears that the involvement of the masses in decisions about patriotism and war does not provide for a better defense of the real interest of most of the people; the issues at stake are subject to mood and rhetoric, which ultimately determine whether and for what and for how long there shall be war. So democracy also works against restraint.

A further escalation from the same period changes the notion of justified revolution. What can count as "just cause" escalates; the claims are stronger and less subject to critical challenge.

The revolutions of the 18th century had talked about "freedom" in ways whose ideological component was simple enough: whether "the people" removed a monarchical government in their own country, as in France, or took their country out from under an empire, as in the American Revolution. There is a quantitative and in fact a qualitative escalation when the "total" ideological claim behind a revolution is not simply an appeal to "freedom" or "the people," but to some more profound basis for the authority to destroy one regime for the sake of a more righteous one, or even to sacrifice one's own people for the sake of a better future order. The major revolutions of the 20th century, whether of the right or of the left, have claimed a higher level of metaphysical validation and therefore are even more difficult to evaluate in terms of moral discourse. In typological terms they become not "just" but "holy" wars.

This is the case for the ideological claims of Marxism when it claims to have risen above the need for moral validation. It may also be the case when "the defense of the free world" is considered to be unquestionable and unchallengeable as a justification for anything that a nation's government claims it has a mandate to do.

Military necessity

The concept of "military necessity"—of being justified, "if you really have to," in doing things that otherwise would be wrong—is introduced as a further source of distance between morality and legality. For strict constructionists like Francis Lieber, the concept of "necessity" is a restriction; even among the kinds of damage which the rules of war permit, one may only inflict those which are indispensable to winning. Lieber's General Orders No. 100, Article 14 (1863) states,

> Military necessity, as understood by modern civilized nations, consists in the necessity of those measures which are indispensable for securing the ends of the war, and which are lawful according to the modern law and usages of war.

The drift is strong toward the permissive use of the notion, however, so that "necessity" comes to mean that one should break the rules only when one really has to: and even that "really has to" tends to boil down to utility rather than emergency.[1] This more flexible understanding of "necessity" is not in itself a new development; yet all the above developments heighten its power.

Other dimensions of uncontrollability

All our attention to the nuclear threshold since 1945 has hidden from many people another qualitative change that was just as fundamental in essence, and in fact more real, since wars of this new kind were really happening. The war in Algeria in 1955-1962 (or that in Vietnam waged by the French in the 1950s and the Americans in the 1960s) was, at least in its intensity and its breadth, a new phenomenon.

Guerrilla war is morally problematic on the revolutionary side, because those who prosecute the war can-

40

not, almost by definition, prove objectively that they are the "legitimate authority" representing the people. They have to accredit themselves by appeal to the cause they represent, to the social or political doctrine they will implement. In early phases of any revolutionary effort they must whip their own people into line with terrorism or at least very stern internal enforcement. They make enemies of their own compatriots who have not yet joined the liberation forces, and thereby undermine rather than strengthen their claim to legitimacy.

On the counterinsurgency side, antiguerilla warfare is also qualitatively harder to justify. Usually the government being defended would itself not be supported by its subjects in a plebiscite. Often, as was the case in Vietnam, it is internally corrupt, politically without vision, and economically or even militarily the puppet of outside forces.

Thus those just-war criteria are selected that are most easily transposed into a less demanding set of rules that can be kept. Others are tacitly neglected because their measurement would be impossible or their enforcement difficult, or because it was not clear that both parties to the treaty would have an equal interest in accepting the restriction.

Even one of the above changes is sufficient to make the applicability of the JWT questionable. When taken cumulatively, they have hollowed out the tradition to little more than a shell. The words are still there, but the realities to which they apply escape almost entirely the discipline which used to be, if not effective, at least reasonably thinkable. The shell has been retained, while what goes on beneath it is something quite different from what the theologians who initially found the JWT convincing could ever have meant or would ever have approved.

4

Hopes for Limiting War

Concurrent with the foregoing developments and interlocking in complicated ways with them are some other changes that do tend to move toward making restraint possible. None of these developments has quite the scale or effectiveness of the degenerative changes summarized in the previous chapter. Yet they are intrinsically valuable and provide some base for keeping the vision alive.

The cosmopolitan vision

While Europe was breaking apart into a chaos of independent principalities and ultimately a score of nation states, gradual progress in education and communication gave meaning to the Renaissance vision of Europe as one *humane* community. Though Erasmian cosmopolitanism was the vision of very few people, it nonetheless retained high visibility and prestige as an alternative vision condemning the way things were going and proclaiming that it could be otherwise. Rulers like King George of Bohemia (peace plan, 1454), humanists like Erasmus (d. 1536), educators like Comenius (*Angel of Peace*, 1667), philosophers like Kant (*Perpetual Peace*, 1795), reformers like William Penn (*Essay Toward the Present and Future Peace of Europe*, 1693), and writers like Victor

Hugo (1849) projected visions of a European parliament possessing the moral power to mediate and arbitrate most conflicts — and if necessary to wield the military sanctions to put down the rest. Never a real possibility, this vision remained alive as a confession of impotence with visible moral power.

Systematic ethics

The next development is best represented by the Jesuit Francisco de Vitoria (d. 1546), writing in the face of the Iberian occupation of South America. Although, as we have seen, the JWT had by then been around for a millennium, it had remained only an implicit moral system, represented in the early Fathers only by scattered fragments and sentences, in canon law only by occasional cases, and in the high Middle Ages only by a few paragraphs amidst other kinds of material in a *Summa*. Not until Vitoria do we find an entire treatise and the development of a coherent and full system trying to speak to numerous major issues in a way that is consistent from point to point and defended against alternative views. Since the Spanish and Portuguese presence in South America was the nearest thing to a crusade in the 16th century, Vitoria's clarification of the just-war tradition also meant the progressive disentanglement, in logic and in practice, of the justifiable-war, properly so-called, from the holy war and from the justification of empire as propagation of true religion. This disentanglement from the crusade was also worked through on other grounds, less thoroughly, by the Protestant reformers, especially Luther, but Vitoria's doing it within systematic ethics was to be of more abiding importance.

Response to "pragmatism"

The move to disentangle the just war from the crusade was also simultaneous with defenses against the naked "reason of state." Thanks to Machiavelli, moral thinkers could not avoid the challenge put to them by his cynical realism. In denouncing him and his moral relativism or opportunism, they likewise restored, if not specifically the just-war ideas, at least in a wider sense the concept that moral accountability is applicable even to princes.

Law of nations

We have been talking thus far about ethicists, people whose connection to the world of political decision was only indirect, and whose language, if it applied at all, worked only on the minds of others who took their guidance before the decision or heard their reprimands after the offense. The next highly significant development was the transposition from the language of morality into the language of law.

Hugo Grotius (d. 1645) has become the symbolic representative of this transition. The law of nations in the modern sense is usually dated from Grotius' systematizing the laws of war. The moral criteria unfolded by the theologians were transposed into the language of the diplomat and the lawyer, so that they might serve as a basis for negotiation and litigation. This was the age when diplomacy was becoming an orderly, expert profession. The increasing importance of sea travel, colonization, and piracy made imperative the creation of a legal system that most nations most of the time would have an interest in respecting and even in helping one another to enforce.

Grotius began his writings as a philosopher and theologian, needing to argue (against cynics and Machiavellians) the case that there was such a thing as moral obligation that is not suspended when war is begun, and that such obligation can and should be respected by leaders, notwithstanding the price in terms of national interest. It was to be a long time before this network of legal ideas became enforceable in some way other than the voluntary compliance of the governments of modern European nations with the terms of bilateral agreements, but the foundation had been laid. From this precedent could grow a body of tradition defining duties incumbent

44

on sovereign nations in their dealings with one another, even though the question of their enforceability became moot in the most important conflicts.

In the process of translation or transposition from morality to law, many elements of the classical thought pattern are easily translated: the dignity of the noncombatant is definable in both frames of reference, as is the notion of a righteous cause. Yet there are significant changes in the tone. A moral principle is generally stated with a view to the restraint it seeks to exercise: the law is more often formulated in terms of how much it can permit. In law, prohibition is implemented by punishment. A hiatus is introduced between what is sinful and what will actually be prosecuted, or between what is immoral and what is prohibited by laws, or between what is prohibited in the words of the law and what prohibitions will actually be enforced. It becomes clear that the reason one party can promise to keep the rules they have written into a treaty is that *if* the other parties also agree, then both sides will gain by fighting fairly. This opens, or sharpens, further questions:

1. What if the other party does not fight fairly? Are we then released from our obligation? (We shall return to this.)

2. Is the obligation based only on the moral reciprocity of its being ultimately in our own interest?

3. Does the obligation defined by a treaty apply only to the parties who have signed the treaty? Or is it understood that what the treaty defines is a natural obligation that applies to all?

4. Do the obligations defined in the treaty apply when the adversary has not signed the treaty? Or are we authorized to disregard treaty obligations toward nonsignatories as "beyond the pale"?

International agencies

The end of the same period also saw the development of international treaties following just-war concepts.

The visions of Grotius took on contractual form. Beginning with the Paris declaration on maritime law (1856) and the Red Cross convention on the wounded (Geneva, 1864), the development continued with St. Petersburg on explosive projectiles (1868), and Brussels (1874), and culminated in the Hague (1899, 1907). In keeping with the selfish interests of Europe's nations, a network of treaties began to move hesitantly toward a small approximation of the world federalist vision. The slow progress in building institutions consistent with the just-war mentality has moved forward, although not as rapidly as the escalation of new threats.

These treaties first began as a "concert of Europe" with the thought that the only ones bound to fight fairly according to these new rules would be those parties who had signed them, so that the rules did not need to be respected when fighting against someone who did not respect them or who was not committed to doing so.

Increasingly, however, the regulations of the Brussels, Hague, and Geneva conventions came to be seen as something all nations should respect, even though some nations did not incorporate these rules in their own domestic enforcement.

The series of treaties grew again after World War I— The Hague (1922), Geneva (1929), London (1936), Geneva (1949)—until the formation of the United Nations as a permanent forum for more such negotiation. Some of these treaties committed their signers to some kind of enforcement mechanism; most did not, but they provided a grid for the internal discipline of those decision makers who wanted to fight fairly. In the United States, these treaties when ratified became law for our soldiers.

Not only does the United Nations organization negotiate new treaties and conventions regulating war, but it and other such agencies are beginning, though feebly, to develop instruments of mediation and arbitration to resolve conflicts which otherwise might have caused a war. The stronger these resources become, the less likely is the situation of "last resort" to be reached.

Codes of combat

It is yet another step from law to military procedure. Ever since the medieval manuals for etiquette of knights and princes, there has been a code of honor for the behavior of those who have the right to bear weapons, especially with regard to the immunity of noncombatants, but it was not until the 19th century that these codes were applied to the common soldier. They then became enforceable as a matter of military discipline and stated in operational terms the obligations laid on soldiers in the field.

These regulations were clarified in the American Civil War, when there was an awareness that the people on the other side, also, were human beings who had certain rights. The immigrant German jurist Francis Lieber was entrusted by the northern secretary of war with the codification of General Orders No. 100 (1863), the grandfather of modern military codes. From that point on it began—only very gradually and imperfectly—to be possible to hold a particular soldier or field officer accountable for his infringement of the rules of fair combat.

Beginning to set a limit

The total wars of Napoleonic Europe and between the American states had marked a threshold in destructiveness. It was no surprise, then, that they also provoked the first critical reaction from the Roman Catholic bishops in their capacity as moral shepherds in the West. The ecumenical council convened at the Vatican in 1870 had on its agenda proposals to declare that modern warfare had become so disproportionate in scale and indiscriminate in targeting that the requirements of the just-war tradition could no longer be met. The council never got to that subject, for two reasons: its concentration on the definition of papal infallibility, and its premature conclusion due to the outbreak of the Franco-Prussian War and the invasion of the Vatican State. Nonetheless it is testimony to the objectivity of the doctrine that thoughts of applying it to "modern war" preceded Hiroshima.

The Berlin University pastor Franciscus Stratmann, who at the outset of World War I supported the German cause, came to honest dissent before 1918 and remained from then until his death in 1971 the primary European spokesman for the unacceptability of modern war according to Catholic teaching. He was removed from his campus chaplaincy in 1917 but was never formally silenced by the Catholic episcopacy.

Beginning with Benedict XV during World War I, we find this moral insight transposed into pastoral preaching on the part of the popes. Benedict inaugurated the pattern, which Pius XII was to renew during World War II, of addressing a message to the world every Christmas that centered on an appeal to peace—an appeal that came from within the just-war tradition. I have elsewhere described this "pastoral" quality of papal pleading for peace as politically weak but nonetheless morally significant.[1] Never, in either the First World War or the Second, did a pope intervene to tell the faithful in any one country that their war was unjust, as the doctrine theoretically would have enabled him to do. Nonetheless the very existence of the papacy, symbolizing the definition in the minds of Catholic Christians of the transnational unity of the Roman Catholic Church, kept the issue of the moral validity of international hostilities more alive in Catholic minds than it was for many Protestants.

It is thus not only the intellectual rigor of Catholic moral thought but also the abiding Catholic sense of supranational community which brought it about that the next step forward in concretizing the tradition was also made by Catholics.

An article by the Jesuit John C. Ford, published in 1944 in the Jesuit journal *Theological Studies,* has been widely referred to as a landmark in the debate about the legitimacy of the massive aerial bombing of cities in World War II. The status, courage, and visibility of Ford earned this recognition, but his position was not original. Most of what Ford argued in 1944 had already been written in 1933 in a Catholic University of America doctoral thesis by John Kenneth Ryan.

The argument is simple. The last years of World War I had made it clear that in the next war there would be massive bombing of cities. Disarmament negotiations between 1918 and 1933 had already reinforced the awareness of how destructive this would be and how difficult it would be to control. Ryan therefore had all the information needed to see the scale of the new moral problem. Even if, under the impact of the notion of "total war," we grant that many people on the other side who are not soldiers are enemies (whether on the grounds of their will or of their active contribution to the war effort), there still are great numbers of the civilian population in cities under enemy administration who continue to belong literally in the category of "innocent." There is no moral justification for tactics of aerial warfare that threaten or take the lives of these people.

Ryan, followed by Ford, looked as well at the ancient Catholic logic of "double effect," whereby it had long been considered permissible to do deeds which one recognized to be in some sense "materially evil," i.e., causing harm, at the same time that one holds them to be justified by other good results which they seek and obtain. Ryan and Ford did not set this argument aside as unworthy, as many critics since Pascal have done, nor did they transpose it into a more refined utilitarianism, as some Catholics in our day are doing. Assuming its legitimacy, they carefully demonstrated that it cannot possibly apply to the kind of case and to the scale of destruction which would have to be defended if the double-effect ideas were seriously applied to cities. They seem, however, to have had practically no influence on the attitudes of the wider Catholic community before the impact of Hiroshima.

In Britain more than in the United States this issue became a matter of public debate. The journalist George Orwell was one of the main voices opposing the just-war restraints against killing civilians. On the other side there were numerous pacifists who used just-war language in the hope of convincing nonpacifists that such destructiveness could not be morally acceptable. There were debates between the Royal Air Force, whose General Harris was more open to obliteration bombing, and the United States Air Force, whose General Arnold was more committed to trying to respect the traditional disciplines of military targeting. Some of the same debate was carried on in Parliament and the councils of the Church of England, with Bishop Bell of Chichester standing against and Archbishop Temple of Canterbury in favor of city bombing.

In all of this renewal of just-war concern the focus was on only one of the many classical criteria: the immunity of noncombatant personnel. It was held that this one criterion was sufficiently powerful to eliminate one particular kind of strategy. This argument was never seriously refuted in its claim to be the imperative application of the tradition. Those who chose not to be bound by it recognized that they were choosing not to be bound by the constraints of the tradition. They claimed the ground of military necessity, which was held to be especially extreme in this circumstance because of the dramatic dimensions of the Nazi threat.

By no means were they taking a position which they granted was less moral. They simply argued that the tradition was not morally adequate at this point. If Hitler truly threatened the survival of the entire value system of Western freedoms, one did not have to respect all the rules when fighting against him. If one could end a war more quickly by not keeping all the rules developed in an earlier tradition, the total cost might on balance be less than dragging out the war by fighting according to earlier, less realistic rules.

The nuclear hurdle

As we noted concerning the Roman Catholic bishops in 1870 and Franciscus Stratmann in 1918, it is important that Ryan and Ford, Arnold and Bell stated their objections in this way *before* the conscience of the world was shaken by the step across the atomic threshold. Nonetheless it was that step which convinced a far greater public that there must be a stopping point.

There is room for debate about whether the atomic threshold is really crucial in every respect. The total amount of damage done at Hiroshima was not immeasurably more than the lives and property destroyed by the firestorm ignited by the bombing of Tokyo a few weeks earlier, or Dresden and Hamburg, although the added dimensions of radiation effects and worldwide fallout need to be weighed against the greater destruction of life and property at Tokyo. But in any case a psychological threshold was crossed, even if in the future that threshold may be whittled down to become more like a gradual scale from "conventional" to nuclear levels of destruction.

To the question of immunity, i.e., naming particular categories of people who ought not to be destroyed, there was clearly added the question of proportionality, i.e., the quantitative measure of the total amount of damage done as measured by comparison to the damage by the other side or other states in the war. How the proportionality was meant to be measured is something the ancient traditions were never clear about, but at least an enormous escalation of destructive potential makes any rational person ask if there must not be a limit somewhere. It makes a logical difference, but hardly a moral one, whether the nuclear threshold be identfied as immunity, proportion, or discrimination.[2]

Such a limit was first stated by the military scientist Commander Sir Stephen King-Hall, who, just a week after Hiroshima, wrote in his professional newsletter that development of this new category of weaponry had to put an end to the possibility of full-scale war between major powers on purely technical military grounds. He expanded his argument into a book, *Defense in a Nuclear Age* (1958), initiating a line of military thinkers who reject current military strategies on grounds of the morality and legality of just war, but also on the grounds of technical military feasibility.

It is this idea that "there must be a limit somewhere" which in the 1950s came to be labeled "nuclear pacifism." This view is generally not linked with firm quantitative argument about just where that limit is, but is convinced that an all-out nuclear exchange (or, of course, an all-out unilateral strike against an enemy population center) would be illicit.

Such a limit was stated by a study commission convened by the World Council of Churches under the heading *Christians and the Prevention of War in a Nuclear Age* (1957), and in similar ways by Pope John XXIII in his encyclical letter *Pacem in Terris* (1963). Theologians Paul Ramsey and Helmut Gollwitzer were among the first and strongest of many Protestant moral thinkers saying the same thing.

As Bryan Hehir wrote (*Commonweal,* March 13, 1981), "A strong and solid consensus has formed against any use of nuclear weapons however limited." Hehir said this, however, in the context of a wider report which made clear that secular political thinkers are moving away from rather than toward that consensus as they seek to widen the room for usable nuclear arms. Thus careful just-war thinkers, like pacifists, are stating positions on fundamental moral grounds without the certainty that they can be effectively implemented with the assent of the people who make the political choices.

Nuremberg

Even before the successful conclusion of World War II, the Allies had decided not only that they would claim the rights of victors to reorder the postwar world, but that they would punish the persons guilty of crimes committed in the prosecution of the war. For our purposes we may let the name of Nuremberg stand as representative of the entire process. It was in that south-German city that the Allies established an impressive procedure wherein judges from the Soviet Union, Britain, France, and the United States tried those accused of crimes both against peace and against the laws of war. Other criminals were tried elsewhere, for example, in France. There was a tribunal as well for offenses committed by Japanese in the Pacific Theater, but its conclusions were not as persuasive. The Indian member dissented.

Discussion continues as to the legal and moral dimensions of the Nuremberg prosecution. This justice was enforced by the victors on the vanquished. Some consider that fact in itself unfair; others point out that that is the nature of all legal conflict. There were important discrepancies among the several legal traditions appealed to for explaining the jurisdiction of the court and the validity of the definitions of crime to be used. Nonetheless the trials provide institutional demonstration for the claim that it is morally and legally incumbent on persons other than sovereigns to refuse to obey an unjust order.

Nuremberg shows that one may be prosecuted later for having failed to disobey an unjust order, *if* one's nation is later defeated. It thereby constitutes a symbolic statement by the victors, in that the distinction they make between those losers whom they prosecute and those who are not prosecuted is based on the classical laws of war. That Nuremberg exonerated some people is just as important for the rule of law as the fact that it condemned some. Thus the fundamental notions of just-war legality were reinforced, even though the prospect of such enforcement after a war would hardly function powerfully to restrain anyone otherwise inclined to commit a war crime in the interest of increasing his chances of winning or in the prosecution of an ideological war.

The trials at Nuremberg were nonetheless not a wasted effort. They were, for instance, appealed to by a few political scientists and lawyers in the American Vietnam debate as having established legal precedent, within the American system, for persons whose disobedience to

American authority was based on the conviction that illegal action was being asked of them.[3]

The responsible citizen draftee

We observed that war had become "total" in its involvement of entire populations with the destruction; now we must turn back to another dimension of modernity, namely the idea of citizen responsibility. Medieval thought did not know the concept of citizen responsibility. Theologians around 1200 said a vassal was not obligated to aid his lord in an unjust war, but they did not declare it his duty to refuse to serve. The prince, not the vassal, was to blame for the injustice. It has been logically possible ever since the Reformation for a soldier or citizen to conclude that a given war was unjustified and therefore to choose to refuse to serve; yet such a development was still unlikely. Martin Luther had already said that if a soldier knew his lord was fighting for an unjust cause, it was the soldier's moral duty to refuse to serve, even at the cost of his life, but very few conscientious Lutherans are reported to have made use of this logical possibility.[4] Rare individuals refused to serve in Hitler's wars on "just war" grounds; most notably the Austrian Catholic Franz Jagerstatter, yet many others who opposed the Hitler regime still accepted military service.

That logical possibility broke through to impressive implementation in the American experience with Vietnam. Considerable numbers of young men refused to serve, for reasons derived not from absolutist pacifism but from their own conscientious, although not always articulate, application of the just-war criteria. They thought the Vietnam hostilities lacked legitimate authority because of their judgment of the South Vietnamese regime or because the presence of American soldiers in combat overseas was not authorized by a formal declaration of war. They considered the means to be improper because of what they had heard about civilian casualties. They considered the cause to be questionable because they gave some credence to the American national vision according to which government is legitimate only with the consent of the governed, and because in their eyes the preservation of a dictatorial regime in Saigon was not a valid purpose for which to fight. Proportionality was questionable; so was winnability. Some of them believed the public rhetoric, according to which the purpose was not the welfare of the citizens of Vietnam, but rather a global conflict between America as center of the free world and communist imperialism on the other side, with Vietnam as simply the turf on which that global battle was to be fought.[5] These applications of the traditional just-war criteria were far more impressive to the ordinary American citizen, whether draftee or voter, than the more demanding traditional pacifist appeals would have been.

Though no way was found for selective-service legislation to recognize this "selective objection" as qualifying for recognition as "conscientious objection," it came in the late 1960s and early 1970s to be formally recognized as a valid moral option by leaders of the major church bodies.[6]

5

The Tradition
and the Real World

As we near the end of our conversation, a few threads can be tied together. This survey will not constitute proof, but will enable readers to understand some preliminary historical conclusions about the status of the just-war tradition as classical consensus.

The scale keeps sliding

The reality of just-war reasoning turns out not only to be more complicated than it sounded at first (it has more levels and subthemes than the usual simple statements make clear), but more important, its fundamental logic is ambivalent. The tradition says that war is generally deplorable and is always in need of being limited, but that there are effective ways to limit it so that those who regretfully have recourse to violence can be assured that what they are doing is not murder. The credibility of this statement, both morally and logically, is tied to the degree to which the defined criteria actually impose effective restraints. Beneath the basic concession that there will have to be some exceptions to the wrongness of killing, we find a set of exceptions to the need for justifications for exceptional killing. The different arguments will carry weight for different people, and they proceed on different levels; yet their cumulative impact is to decrease the credibility of the tradition and the applicability of the stated limits.

1. Lowering the hurdles

Any set of rules will tend to favor the interests of those who wrote the rules. In a context of technical change, they will favor those parties whose strength was greatest in terms of the older techniques. Two examples are obvious in recent strategic history.

    a. The earlier rules defined those who have the right to be considered as soldiers (rather than common criminals or bandits) by their wearing a uniform (or other distinguishing sign) and carrying their arms visibly. Modern times have seen an escalation of the importance of irregular or guerrilla forces (called "terrorists" by their enemies and "freedom fighters" by their friends), whose operation would be rendered practically impossible by respecting those rules. So we need new rules to permit guerrilla war, in order to regulate it.

    b. The earlier rules for submarine warfare, derived from those of surface naval engagement, forbade torpedoing a ship without surfacing to confirm that it was in fact carrying arms. To respect such a rule in World War I was to sacrifice the entire advantage of submarine technology, and to render the German submarines nearly defenseless against the British ruse of placing guns on what looked like unarmed merchant vessels. The victorious allies, stronger in surface technology, reaffirmed the old rules after World War I; but those rules were a dead letter in World War II. In the Nuremberg trials Allied submarine commanders testified in defense of German commanders accused of not respecting those rules, saying that Allied submarines had not respected them either.

These two cases illustrate the principle that rules are more likely to be kept if they are less demanding and more "realistic." One therefore consents to sacrifice the values which the original rules safeguarded in the hope of avoiding complete lawlessness. In the interest of maintaining restraint in a minimal way, one agrees to relax the particular restraints which would really have made it more difficult to continue hostilities and win. It is thought better to have some few modest rules that both sides can afford to keep than more weighty rules that will not be respected.

In this same direction William V. O'Brien has argued that the principle of noncombatant immunity can no longer be effectively respected. Instead of affirming it abstractly by undercutting its real meaning with arguments of necessity and double effect, it would be more appropriate to declare it a dead letter and to concentrate on building up those other restraints that are still realistic.

George Orwell was saying something of the same kind in World War II. It is better to get the war over quickly by whatever means—once you have resolved to accept war at all—rather than let it be strung out and its total destructiveness increased by placing artificial limits on your most effective weapons. When the enemy's troops are draftees, they may well be no less morally "innocent" than the aged. Why should a war be better which kills only healthy young men?

2. "Necessity"

The classic JWT said that the means used should be "necessary and proportionate," as a warning against wanton destruction or any damage not directly functioning toward the goal of winning the war. "Necessity" was then within the limits of the rules. It was so defined by Francis Lieber (1863). It is still so defined in the U.S. Army Field Manual 27-10 of 1956:

> The prohibitory effect of the law of war is not minimized by "military necessity" which has been defined as that principle which justifies those measures not forbidden by international law which are indispensable for securing the complete submission of the enemy as soon as possible. Military necessity has been generally rejected as a defense for acts forbidden by the customary and

conventional laws of war inasmuch as the latter have been developed and framed with consideration for the concept of military necessity.

Yet increasingly the ordinary use of "necessity" has become the opposite; it has come to mean a claimed justification for breaking one or another of the rules—"but only if you *really have to.*" Then the practical meaning of "really have to" depends on the particular value that is at stake at the time: a captain not wanting to jeopardize his men's lives "unnecessarily"; a general not wanting to jeopardize the outcome of a particular battle; a statesman not wanting to prolong "unnecessarily" or to lose a war.

As Telford Taylor and Michael Wasserstrom have pointed out, the practical effect of this shift is to reduce "necessity" to "utility," giving oneself *carte blanche* for any destruction that is not purely wanton or wasteful.[1] Yet this reality is not openly avowed; phrases like "only if it is *really* necessary" still maintain the claim that one is being responsible.

3. "They did it first."

Here again we have a long spectrum of degrees of infraction. The minimum is a specific act of "reprisal" intended to punish the adversary for an infraction and prevent its recurrence. This then calls for continued application of the rules of proportionality and discrimination, and there needs to be a way to communicate with the enemy (as through the Red Cross) so that they know we will do to them what they will do to us and that we will stop if they do. One must infringe on the rules no further than the enemy did, and the intent of the exceptional sanction must be to restore the rules.

A more sweeping abandon of such rules results if one takes more seriously the dimension of contract thinking in the development of the international conventions. What those conventions forbid is not wrong morally and intrinsically; it is wrong conventionally between two parties who, in the interest of both, have agreed to fight by those rules. If, however, the other side breaks the rules, the deal is off and we are no longer bound to them either. If they have marked with a red cross vehicles or buildings used for military purposes, the immunity of their wounded is sacrificed; likewise if they attack our ambulance or hospital. While we still claim to be more moral than they, we descend to fight by their rules.

4. *"They are unworthy."*

The identity of the adversaries whose rights the JWT protects is not clear. On the one hand, it would seem natural that since the rights being protected are those of enemies, it would hardly be fitting to distinguish between those enemies who do and those who do not have such rights. Yet, as the tradition has been applied, there often have been such discriminations. This fact arises from the understanding that the just-war standards are somewhat analogous to the good manners which should exist among the citizens of a civil society; warfare according to the rules is then something like a court process or a duel. In the medieval period many of the limitations on illicit weapons or tactics only forbade their use *against Christians*, assuming that against the infidel another level of destructiveness might be permitted. Thus the wedge between the crusade and the just war properly so-called began as a wedge between two kinds of adversary. The infidel, being beyond the pale of civility, did not possess even those rights which the JWT defended.

In modern times there are also vestiges of the notion that adversaries can put themselves "beyond the pale" and forfeit their rights to be fought against fairly. Sometimes this can be argued on the basis of whether a particular nation has signed a certain treaty. The Afrikaner nationalists facing the British in the Boer War had been claiming independence for decades, but they had not been represented at the drafting of the Hague convention. The British further proclaimed their "annexation" at the outset of the war, holding that the insurgents did not count as a legitimate authority. It was therefore possible for the

British to argue that those rules did not apply to those enemies. Before 1939 Japan had not signed some of the international conventions on the treatment of prisoners of war, because of the assumption that Japanese soldiers would never be taken prisoner. Therefore it could not be demanded of them with force of law that allied prisoners of war in the Asian theater during World War II be dealt with according to those rules.

Just as often, one of the parties is held to be beyond the pale not because of the document they had not signed, but because they broke the rule first, and thereby qualified themselves as outlaws rather than combatants. The right to be fought against according to the laws of war would then, the argument goes, be revocable. A parallel argument rages now in Belfast, in Latin America, and in South Africa, over whether insurrectionists should be treated as political prisoners or as common criminals.

Such escalation of the evil we allow ourselves to commit, on the ground of the special evil incarnate in the adversary, has often seemed convincing, especially when the clash has ideological overtones. The Turks had that image in the Middle Ages; Nazism had it yesterday; and godless communism has it today. Though generally critical of the "sliding scale" logic, Michael Walzer was ready to admit a "supreme" emergency argument in favor of the massive bombing of German cities, because a Nazi victory — more than most losses in war — would have meant the end of certain basic values of Western civilization.[2] I mentioned this before as a specific case of "necessity" reasoning; but for it to be convincing one must have made some previous global judgments about Nazism and civilization. Once more we can discern here a shift from intrinsic morality to contractual thinking. We are not obligated to respect the humanity of the enemy population because they are human, but only because they have committed themselves to carry on the combat according to our rules. If their rulers deny our basic value system, the enemies forfeit the privilege of our respect. It was a privilege which we, being morally superior, had bestowed upon them, or a conditional right which they earned by meeting us on our terrain — not an intrinsic right by virtue of their humanity. "Savages" and "outlaws" have no rights. Thus the worse the enemy's cause, the more room we may have to break the rules too.

5. *Situationism*

Many of the common-sense responses that arise in the effort to move just-war thought past the first phases of apparent "realism" take the shape of anti-intellectual or antistructural reasoning. "In a combat situation there is no time for complicated calculation of possibilities"; or, "When the lives of my men are at stake, philosophy is not very convincing." The normal penchant of the human heart for such excuses is precisely why we need rules. Precisely because there is not much time, decision makers need reminders of the fundamental rights of the other parties in the conflict, which remain even in the midst of unavoidable conflict. Precisely because abstract analysis is not appropriate or easy under fire, the limits of our entitlement to destroy our fellows' lives and property need to be formulated firmly ahead of time so as to be protected against our (partially, but not infinitely) justified self-interest.

6. *Systematize*

Whereas some of the least worthy adjustments, like those just described, use ordinary debating language, and some of them even make a point of representing the realism of the lay person against the more complicated reasoning processes of the specialist, there is one line of argument which claims deep roots in the tradition of the most intellectually careful moral theologians. The doctrine of double effect has a long history, claiming the capacity to throw light on especially difficult choices, in which competing or coinciding values cannot be separated from one another, so that in order to ward off one evil it seems that one must accept another.

Ethicists are far from agreement on the precise interpretation and justification of this pattern of argument, but there is agreement on its basic outlines. One must be able to show that:

a. The evil which happens is less than the evil which is prevented.
b. The evil which happens because of the choice one makes is a by-product of the entire set of events, and is not itself an actual cause of the good results (otherwise one would be doing evil directly for the sake of good, and classically that is not permitted).
c. The evil which occurs should not be willed or intended.
d. The actual deed which both triggers the evil by-product and is indispensable to the good primary intention is not itself intrinsically wrong.[3]

It is not our concern here to argue about the appropriateness of double-effect reasoning. We note only that it constitutes a powerful intellectual argument contributing to the downward drift. Some argue only that the just-war theory as a whole represents a case of double effect, where the killing of enemies is the regrettable and unintended result of the intrinsically good defense of national values. Others, however, use double-effect reasoning on the next lower level: the evil which one regretfully accepts for the sake of a higher good is not the killing itself but the fact that one does it in infraction of one of the just-war criteria. Thus one can speak, for instance, of the acceptance of noncombatant deaths or the use of forbidden weapons or the misuse of Red Cross protection as a lesser evil, not intended but regretfully accepted as a part of the price for a higher good. It is very difficult for the critic who wants to be fair at this point to know where the line runs between careful casuistic good faith and plain cynical abuse.

7. This far and no farther?

The earliest firm landmark in the development of what we have since come to call "nuclear pacifism" was a study process convened by the study department of the World

Council of Churches following its 1954 Evanston Assembly. A group of 14 thinkers, all of them from the North Atlantic world, worked for several sessions on the theme, "Christians and the Prevention of War in an Atomic Age." Of the 14 commission members (in addition to staff from the study department and the Churches' Commission on International Affairs), only three could in any way be spoken of as pacifist.

Their report was far ahead of what Christian bodies in any national or denominational framework were to think for another decade. Their conclusion about the use of nuclear weapons was:

> Although there are differences of opinion on many points, we are agreed on one point. This is that Christians should openly declare that the all-out use of these weapons should never be resorted to. Moreover, that Christians must oppose all policies which give evidence of leading to all-out war. Finally, if all-out war should occur, Christians should urge a cease fire, if necessary on the enemy's terms, and resort to non-violent resistance.[4]

This wording, although logically irreproachable as a statement of the ordinary meaning of the just-war tradition, was so threatening that it provoked a striking series of defensive maneuvers on the part of the World Council of Churches—but that is not our present concern.

The logic of the statement was clear and has never been refuted on its own terrain. If one cannot with moral legitimacy prosecute a war, then the only morally worthy alternative is not to prosecute it. The only remaining path is to pursue by other means the purposes which can no longer be legitimately achieved militarily.

8. Surrender rather than fight?

It is therefore appropriate that we should turn directly to the crudest form of the credibility question: Is there any point at which it would be morally obligatory to surrender rather than to wrongly prosecute a war? Does the doctrine imply that? On the level of common sense and the lay meaning of the JWT, it certainly did—and does—

imply the possibility that the wrongness of a particular cause, or a particular battle, or a particular weapon or tactic is so clear that it must not happen, even at the cost of important sacrifice. This possible negation is a part of the dignity of the tradition. The negation applies most dramatically and globally when one says that if the only way to defend even a just cause is by a fundamentally wrong means, it is mandatory to surrender and seek to pursue further the defense of one's valid interests through means other than the belligerents' defense of national sovereignty. The clearest statements that the just-war tradition has not been applied by the major political powers in recent Western experience have come not from pacifists but from the most qualified interpreters of that tradition. Among the qualified advocates of this implication are the firm statements of Paul Ramsey, the pre-eminent American Protestant author in the field, who opens the same possibility:

> The test is whether we are willing to limit ends and means in warfare and yet sustain the burden of this evil necessity, whether we as a people are willing, if war comes, to accept defeat when our fighters cannot win the hoped-for victory rather than venture more and exact more than the nature of just endurable warfare requires, whether we can mount the resources for action with at most small effect and plan surrender when none is possible.[5]

Another example is John Courtney Murray, S.J., author of numerous writings in the field, whose *Morality and Modern War* was published in 1959. He explains the fact that the doctrine is not trusted on the grounds that Catholics have not used it for so long:

> That is, it has not been made the basis for a sound critique of public policies and as a means for the formation of a right public opinion. The classic example, of course, was the policy of "unconditional surrender" during the last war. This policy clearly violated the requirement of the "right intention" that has always been a principle in the traditional doctrine of war. Yet no sus-

tained criticism was made of the policy by Catholic spokesmen. Nor was any substantial effort made to clarify by moral judgment the thickening mood of savage violence that made possible the atrocities of Hiroshima and Nagasaki. I think it is true to say that the traditional doctrine was irrelevant during World War II. This is no argument against the traditional doctrine. The Ten Commandments do not lose their imperative relevance by reason of the fact that they are violated. But there is place for an indictment of all of us who failed to make the tradition relevant.[6]

Murray was without challenge the most qualified Roman Catholic authority in America in his generation to deal theologically with the political order. He not only let the doctrine speak honestly to condemn what the political authorities of his nation had done; he also drew from it the honest logical conclusion that if the doctrine is to be respected, it must set a limit to what a nation is willing to do in order to win. This must mean concretely defining a point at which it is morally imperative to surrender.

[O]n grounds of the moral principle of proportion the doctrine supports the grave recommendation of the greatest theorist of war in modern times, von Klausewitz: "We must therefore familiarize ourselves with the thought of an honorable defeat."

"Losing," said von Klausewitz, "is a function of winning," thus stating in his own military idiom the moral calculus prescribed by traditional moral doctrine. The moralist agrees with the military theorist that the essence of a military situation is uncertainty. And when he requires, with Pius XII, a solid probability of success as a moral ground for a legitimate use of arms, he must reckon with the possibility of failure and be prepared to accept it. But this is a moral decision, worthy of a man and of a civilized nation. It is a free, morally motivated, and responsible act, and therefore it inflicts no stigma of dishonor.[7]

Murray was no defeatist. He insisted that surrender is not the first but the last possibility. The doctrine of the just war assumes that there can be justifiable ways to wage war. Yet he had the honesty to admit that that entire argument is only sustainable if and as those who hold to it do in fact set a limit beyond which they would abandon the military defense of their goals. That may never mean the annihilation of the enemy, nor need it (in the case of a justifiable war) mean one's own surrender.

> [S]urrender may be morally tolerable; but it is not to be tolerated save on a reasonable calculus of proportionate moral costs. In contrast, annihilation is on every count morally intolerable; it is to be averted at all costs.[8]

It is thus established that for at least some nonpacifists, believing themselves faithful to the just-war tradition, there is a cease-fire line dictated by the doctrine.

The simplest functional definition of the JWT is that one would rather surrender than commit certain belligerent acts. *If the only way not to lose a war is to commit a war crime, it is morally right to lose that war.* If that is intended seriously, there will be moral teaching and contingency planning in preparation for that extreme possibility. If that possibility is not affirmed, the basic moral issue has not yet been faced, and we do not yet know that "necessity" will not be used arbitrarily.

9. Category slide

One of the most frequent ways of undercutting the critical potential of the doctrine is to center only on one or the other of the criteria. Robert Tucker has in fact identified as a specifically American temptation the idea that only the criterion of just cause really matters.[9] We try to stay out of a war until it is clear that someone else is to blame: then our tendency would be to prosecute it without restraint. To put it technically, considerations of *jus ad bellum* are given such a great weight that they override the restraints of *jus in bello*. If the cause that is at stake is great enough, it may be appropriate to disregard some of the ordinary restraints in the prosecution of hostilities.

Responsibility to look at all the criteria can also be evaded in the other direction. Many contemporary thinkers say that it is no longer possible to ask the question of just authority (since the rise of theologies of revolution) nor to ask effectively the question of just cause (since in a situation of absolute national sovereignty every nation is judge over its own case), so that we should limit ourselves to asking in effect only the questions of discrimination: proportionality and immunity. Only those questions of a purely formal character can be asked, because for the others no one can give an answer.

In a backhanded way this argument has some value. It keeps people from saying that since their own cause is just, they need not proceed justly *in bello*. Restraints *in bello* remain valid even for us—if our cause is just— as protection for our opponent's rights — even if their cause is unjust. That does not mean, however, that Christian moral responsibility can avoid the questions of moral evaluation on the levels of authority and cause merely because the other parties to the conflict are obviously biased. The rootage of Christian moral thought — in awareness of the world community, in the thought of the ages, and in the tools of rational critical discourse— should enable asking questions that the other parties to the conflict are not interested in asking. That should continue to include questions of just authority and just cause.

10. *Metamorality*

Thus far we have been moving with the ordinary understanding of the JWT as providing moral guidance for decision makers in government and in combat. The "slide" we have documented was expressed in the "realistic" terms used to justify exceptions and explain tradeoffs on that level. There is however also a more academic level on which the bindingness of the rules can be challenged. James Childress argues that what he calls a "substantive" JWT, which could give concrete guidance, is an impossibility in a society with competing theories of justice. In a pluralistic world people will never agree on what is a just government, a just cause. Therefore there can never be a clear *no* to an unjust war. Yet Childress holds that the tradition is useful. A formal theory provides a common language within which to debate.[10]

There have been dozens of variants within JWT thought in the past. No one can deny Childress the freedom to create yet another. Yet in the measure in which that freedom is taken, he must forsake the claim to be interpreting a classical moral tradition. That the classical tradition (moral and legal) includes the possibility of concrete negative answers regarding the admissibility of specific belligerent acts is evidenced by:

a. The possibility of selective objection and civil disobedience;
b. The prosecution of war crimes;
c. The founding of "just cause" claims and "reprisal" claims in the objective wrongness of offenses committed by the other side;
d. The possibility of "surrender" in the just-war thought of Paul Ramsey, John Courtney Murray, and the World Council of Churches commission.

Other differences, lay or sophisticated, as between the citizen and the politician, the idealist and the realist, can also be appealed to in favor of such relativism. Some restraint is better than none, even if the rules are never fully respected. Of course, it is relatively better for the enemy if we respect only some of the just-war restraints than if we respected none of them at all. But we are now asking not about the greater or lesser disutility of moral killing for its victims; we are concerned for the moral claims of the killers.

All of these arguments belong to the unavoidable complexity of public moral discourse; what is less clear is how they could be thought to heighten rather than to deny the ability of just-war thought to provide moral guidance.

By now the reader will have discerned the drift. The person wanting critically but open-mindedly to give a fair hearing to the claim that the JWT is a usable structure of moral accountability was first of all told that the

69

JWT agrees that war is an evil. Only under the circumstances stated by the criteria evolved over the centuries is that evil justified, because (as the application of all the criteria serves to verify) it is lesser than the evil it prevents. Those criteria guarantee that there is no *carte blanche;* there are some things one would never do, even for a just cause. But then when we ask about the firmness with which the criteria apply, we discover that they keep sliding farther down the scale. With each concession that lowers the line at one point, the claim is renewed that this still does not mean "anything goes":

a. The double effect is still subject to four criteria.
b. Reprisals are still subject to proportionality.
c. Relaxing some rules that submarines cannot keep is done in order to safeguard the idea of law as such.
d. The rules will never be met, but if we keep talking about them there will be fewer infractions than if we don't.
e. It is not perfectly clear what compliance would mean, but at least we have a common vocabulary.

The slippery-slope pattern is undeniable.

Retreats or routs?

Does the tradition lay a reliable foundation for common discussion and possible common decision about admissible levels of damage which political imperatives may oblige responsible decision makers to accept? What seems on closer scrutiny actually to be going on is a sequence of what look at first like strategic retreats but turn out to be routs. A strategic retreat is an act of deciding soberly to step back to a line which may be more firmly defended. That is what *seems* to be happening when someone begins the discussion saying that concessions will need to be made (just this once), but they will only be justified in cases of self-defense, last resort, etc. That sounds like a line that is easier to defend than the prohibition of all killing. But when it comes to defending that line, we discover that there are other reasons being alleged for stepping back still farther:

a. The law must not be made too demanding, or else it will be disrespected.
b. We cannot be obligated to stand by all of the niceties of the rules of war if the enemy does not.
c. Sometimes a situation of very powerful menace may be thought of as a moral equivalent of an attack, so that the best defense is preemptive aggression.

What had looked like a line that could be defended is now becoming a spectrum of degrees of concession to whatever recourse the most pessimistic picture of the conflict enables someone to claim is necessary. What initially looked like a firm structure for moral discernment has turned spongy. What claimed to be (in contrast to the intrinsic moral values of pacifism or the holy war) an instrumentarium of resources for fine-tuned discrimination turns out in the majority of cases we can find in the literature to have been special pleading.

When we give the just-war system a chance to prove its integrity, to prove that a strategic retreat was authentically that by being able more effectively to hold the new lower line, it fails to deliver.

The reasoning is really different

The just-war position is not the one which has been taken practically by most Christians since Constantine. Most Christians (i.e., most baptized people) in most wars since Christians forsook pacifism have died and killed in the light of thought patterns which derive from the crusade or the national-interest pattern. Some have sought to cover and interpret this activity with the rhetoric of the just-war tradition; many have not bothered. The just-war tradition remains dominant as a consensus of the stated best insights of the spiritual and intellectual elite, using that language as a tool for moral leverage on sovereigns for whom the language of gospel has carried no

71

conviction. Thus the just-war rhetoric and radical pacifism are on the same side of the debate: both wish when honest to reject most wars, most causes, most strategies being prepared for and used.

How then could the notion that the JWT is the mainstream position remain alive at all? Certainly it is not only that people were misled as to the power of theologians to get a hearing. Certainly there have been both ideal visions and real models of Christian statesmanship and civil heroism. There have been people who in the exercise of public responsibility with restraint, wisdom, and magnanimity saved or created nations, kept the violence and the bloodthirstiness of war from getting out of hand, and made peace through power. The closer one comes to the domestic model, where restrained violence is like that of the police officer, the more applicable is just-war language, and the more credible is its claim to provide real guidance. Thus people who incarnate domestic order and who succeed in imposing social peace from positions of power may have more to do with making believable the idea of violence with restraint than do actual experiences in war between nations.

The faith was often different

The just-war tradition is not dominant in practice: neither is it dominant in spirituality. When the history of ethical thought is based on the writings of an intellectual elite, then it is the just-war tradition that must be reported. But how many people like that were there, and how many more people were there who drew spiritual sustenance from them?

If, on the other hand, we were to ask how through the centuries most people—who were in some authentic sense Christian believers and lived their life of faith with some explicit sincerity—thought about war, then we should have to report that their lives were nourished not by the *summas* of the schoolmen but by the stories of the saints. Most of the saints were nonviolent. Practically all of those saints who attained to that status through martyrdom were explicitly nonviolent. The rejection of violent self-defense or service in the armies of Caesar was sometimes a part of why they were martyred. The lives of the saints are told in such a way as to incite the hearer to trust God for one's surviving and prospering. Even those saints who lived in the midst of some war and those few who were warriors were not Machiavellian. They cultivated a world view marked by trusting God for one's survival and by the utter absence of utilitarian cynicism in their definition of the path of obedience. The penitent and the pilgrim were normally, naturally defenseless. The stories of the saints abounded in tales of miraculous deliverances from the threats of bandits and brigands.

It is a source of deep historical confusion to identify the history of Christian morality with the record of the thoughts of academic moralists. Such academic elaboration may in some cultures, but not in all, make a major contribution to how people will actually make decisions in the future—if local preachers or confessors take their cues from the professor. But in other traditions, where the instrument of enforcement that the confessional provides is not used, the relation between the academic articulation and the real life of the community is more like that of the froth to the beer.

6

Making the Tradition Credible

This review of ups and downs should have made it clear that the just-war tradition is not a simple formula needing only to be applied in some self-evident and univocal way. It is rather a set of very broad assumptions, whose implications demand—if they are to be respected as morally honest—that they be spelled out in some detail and then tested for their ability to throw serious light on real institutions and institutional decisions.

We turn now to the effort to itemize the resources that would be needed if such implementation were to become a reality.

Intention

Beginning from the inside, we would need to clarify whether in the minds and the hearts of the people using this language there has been a conscious commitment to the willingness to pay the price of the refusal which becomes imperative when the doctrine applies negatively. At some time (if the doctrine is not a farce) there cannot fail to be cases where an intrinsically just cause would have to go undefended because there would be no authority legitimated to defend it, or when an intrinsically just cause defended by a legitimate authority would have to be lost because the only way to defend it would be by unjust means. Then it would be tested whether citizens or leaders are able in principle to conceive of the sacrifice of that value as morally imperative. Is it something citizens would press upon their leaders? Is it reason for the draftee to refuse to serve, or reason for a statesman to lead his people in negotiating peace?

There is no valid ground for believing that most people using just-war language are ready for that serious choice, either psychically or intellectually. In popular language—which translates "negotiated peace" as "surrender" and which proclaims that "there is no substitute for victory"—and in the loose use of the language of "military necessity" to cover almost any infraction of the laws of war, we see the signals not simply of the high value attributed uncritically to one's nation or to the righteousness of one's cause, but a profound psychodynamic avoidance mechanism. By refusing to face real options, that avoidance makes it less likely that in undesirable situations there will be any chance of making the best of a bad deal.

Last resort

What constitutes a situation of last resort is not something which will be decided only at the last minute. In the resolution or failure to resolve political conflicts by less destructive means, what is likely to be decisive is whether such means were planned for in the first place. When for the first decade after Hiroshima the United States counted on its nuclear monopoly to enable us to keep the peace around the globe, there was not sufficient quantity of nonnuclear military means to use in smaller conflicts, so that the recourse to the nuclear threat ("massive retaliation") threatened to be not the last but the only resort. The United States has been less willing than some other nations to accept the authority of agencies of international arbitration, with the Connally Amendment actually undercutting in a formal way the possibility of recourse to agencies like the Hague International Court of Justice.

Even less have we invested in means of conflict resolution on still lower levels. We have shared with the Soviet Union the strategy of escalating local conflicts into surrogates for superpower confrontation, rather than seeking to maximize the authentic independence of nonaligned nations and groups.

The economic patterns dominating our country have militated against the possible use of economic and cultural sanctions (positive and negative) to foster international goals. Few politicians would have the courage, and our legal system would hardly have the authority, to enforce an economic blockade. And our international aid agencies would hardly have the expertise to administer positive reinforcement in such a way as to diminish recourse to military sanctions. We have agencies like the CIA which contribute to escalating rather than diminishing tension when a government overseas raises any question about our national interests. If we sought to be honest about the restraint on violence implied in the just-war tradition, we would have a nonviolent alternative to the CIA, which instead of destabilizing unfriendly regimes would find positive means of fostering more friendly development.

Strategies of nonviolence

We have already given attention to the possibility of recourse to international agencies of arbitration and mediation as a new factor in evaluating when a situation of "last resort" exists. More attention needs to be given, and has only begun to be given, to another new development in our age: the rise of nonviolent strategies for social conflict and change. The impact of Gandhi and King, especially in the Anglo-Saxon world, is only the tip of the iceberg. Beside and beyond them have also been:

1. Great numbers of spontaneous phenomena of noncooperation with injustice, which have achieved some-

times the desired social change and sometimes a more powerful witness of martyrdom than lashing out violently would have;

2. A growing circle of leaders, using similar tactics in their most varied circumstances;

3. A growing body of political science literature projecting the serious possibility of doing, without military violence, some of the things which have been previously claimed could be done only by war. Nonviolent action on behalf of justice is no automatic formula with promise of success: but neither is war. After all, at least half of the people who go to war for some cause deemed worthy of it are defeated.

A careful reading of history can find far greater reasons than many people have previously thought for expecting nonviolent strategies to be effective. Beyond this, however, both experience and the social-science literature have made a good beginning toward projecting and evaluating possible nonmilitary means for defending those values which military means can no longer defend, either practically or morally.

This present study cannot review, digest, or evaluate that literature. For present purposes it suffices to take note of its presence. If a body of thought and a set of tools of analysis and projection have been developed which respond seriously to the question, "How can we defend ourselves if war can no longer do it?" then the situation of last resort may not yet be assumed to obtain. Most of these thinkers are not pacifist: notable among the early ones was Commander Stephen King-Hall, instructor in military science in both the Army and Navy War Colleges of Great Britain during World War II.[1] Those who would consider themselves pacifists are often not committed religiously or absolutely: the arguments they use and the recourses they propose do not presuppose an integrally pacifist value commitment. For their arguments to hold water it suffices to agree that war is not justified when it does not achieve its stated aims and when it does more harm than good.

If there are more nonviolent resources available than people have thought about, and if there would be still more such means available if they were to be thought about more (which is certainly the case elsewhere in human experience, and certainly the case in the realm of violence), then the conclusion is unavoidable that the notion of last resort—one of the classical criteria of the JWT—must exercise more restraint than it did before.

Authority

The next logical test of the mental readiness of people to live with the limits of honest just-war reasoning is the institutional one. The American government invests millions of staff hours and billions of dollars in developing contingency plans for all possible situations in which the legitimate military prosecution of hostilities would be effective. Where is the contingency planning, where are the thought exercises and training maneuvers for continuing the defense of our values in those situations where military means will not be appropriate? Over 20 years ago King-Hall projected the case for *Defense in a Nuclear Age* needing to be, in at least some cases, nonmilitary. It cannot be held that the refusal to respond to that challenge was based on the author's not being competent or respected or his arguments not being cogent. Whether the avoidance mechanisms are best analyzed in budgetary, personality-political, or psychodynamic terms, in any case they discredit the honesty of those who refuse to respond to him, and thereby discredit also the credibility of their *pro forma* adherence to the laws of war.

This statement was backhanded: I should state the affirmation which corresponds to it. The "just authority" which claims the right and the duty to defend the legitimate interests of its citizens or its allies by the disciplined and proportionate use of military violence, will be morally credible only when it gives evidence of a proportionate investment of creativity and foresight in arrangements to defend those same values in those other contexts in which military means would not be morally or legally or technically appropriate. If they are not making those contingency plans, then both their claim that they had a right and duty to defend those values and their claim that they do it within the moral limits of the just-war heritage and the legal limits of the laws of war are not credible.

This reference to contingency planning for alternative strategies, which could be a proof of sincerity, yields another benefit for our conversation. It tells us that in the measurement of what constitutes "last resort" it is not morally sufficient for politicians or strategists to shrug their shoulders and say "we didn't think of anything else"; at least in modern times we have the social-science instruments and intellectual discipline for thinking of alternatives. Last resort can only be claimed when other resorts short of the last have been faced seriously.

Proportion

The reasoning process required by the JWT calls for the evil likely to be caused by warfare to be measured against the evil it hopes to prevent. The critics of the tradition have always wondered what kind of reasoning is going on when one measures various kinds of goods and evils against each other: lives against freedoms, institutions against architecture. We are however trying now to wager on the credibility of the tradition: those who believe that this thought pattern is reliable owe it to their own dignity (and to the right to live of their victims) to have reliable and verifiable measures of the evil they claim to be warding off and the lesser evil they are ready to commit, although reluctantly and without direct intention.

Such calculation must properly seek to take account not only of specific deeds that one is immediately aware of choosing, but also of the potential for escalation and proliferation of the violent effects. It would be appropriate as well that one should factor in the greater or lesser degree of certainty with which one is predicting both kinds of evils or the ability to achieve the just-cause results. Certainly decisions based on the claimed ability to bring about proportionally less evil results, and to do so at the expense of the values and lives of others, need for the sake of one's own integrity to be tested. Such proportionality reckoning can never be certain, but the burden of proof is with the party who says that it is probable enough to justify intervening by causing some evils in order to reduce other projected evils.

Moral leverage

Thus far I have been describing what political instruments and structures would be needed to make the doctrine credible from the perspective of applicability. Another set of questions, however, properly comes first, from the perspective of the religious community. It might also very well be the only angle from which governmental progress could be fostered. Are there people who claim that their own uncoerced allegiance as religious believers prepares them to help one another respect the meaning of the JWT—at the operational point of defining when a citizen would enter the opposition, a government bureaucrat would be obliged to resign, or a soldier would become a selective conscientious objector? Does the church teach future soldiers and citizens so that they will know beyond what point they cannot support an unjust war or use an unjust weapon?

Since the ability to reach an independent judgment concerning the morality of what is being done by one's rulers depends on information, does the religious community provide alternative resources for gathering and evaluating information concerning the political causes for which their governments will ask for their violent support? What are the preparations being made to obtain and verify an adequately independent and reliable source of perspective and facts, permitting honest dissent to be so solidly founded as to be morally convincing?

Is every dissenter on his own, or will the churches support agencies to foster dissent when called for?

Are the soldiers when assigned a mission given sufficient information to determine whether this is an order they should obey? It is reported that in the case of the obliteration bombing of Dresden the pilots were not informed that it could hardly be considered a military target.

Neither the pacifist nor the crusader needs to study at great depths the facts of politics. The person claiming to respect the just-war rationality must do so, and therefore must have an independent, credible source of information. Is there free debate? Is opposition legitimate? Does the right to conscientious disobedience have legal recognition?

Until now church agencies on any level have invested little effort in literature or other educational instruments to teach the understanding of just-war limitations. The few such efforts are in no way comparable to the way in which the churches do teach their young people about other matters concerning which they believe Christian morality is important, such as sexuality.[2] The understanding of the just-war logic which led American young men to refuse to serve in Vietnam came to them not primarily from the ecclesiastical or academic interpreters of the just-war tradition but rather from the notions of fair play which are presupposed in the western and police thriller.

A fair test

Those who move, either immediately or less rapidly, to the claim that in a given situation of injustice there are no nonviolent options available, generally do so in a way that avoids responsibility for an intensive search for other options. The military option for which they reach so soon involves a very long lead time; it demands the preparation of leadership people by special training, educational institutions, and experiences; it demands financial and technical resources dependent on extensive government funding in a situation of defense; and it demands broad alliances. It includes the willingness to lose lives and to take lives, the willingness to sacrifice other cultural values for a generation or longer, the willingness of families to be divided.

Yet the decision that "nonviolence will not work" for analogous ends is made without any comparable investment of time or creativity, without comparable readiness to sacrifice, without serious projection of comparative costs. The American army could not "work" if we did not invest billions of dollars in equipping it and in preparing for its effective use. Why should it be fair to measure the moral claims of an alternative moral strategy by setting up the debate in such a way that that other strategy must produce comparable results at incomparably less cost? The epigram of the 1960s—"People give nonviolence two weeks to solve their problems, and then say it has 'failed'; they've gone on with violence for centuries, and it seems never to have 'failed'"—is not a pacifist argument, but a self-corrective within just-war reasoning.

In sum: the challenge ought to be clear. If the tradition which claims that war may be justified does not also admit that it could be unjustified, the affirmation is not morally serious. A Christian who prepares the case for a justified war without being equally prepared for the negative case has not soberly weighed the *prima facie* presumption that any violence is wrong until the case for an exception has been made. We honor the moral seriousness of the nonpacifist Christian when we spell out the criteria by which the credibility of that seriousness must be judged.

Notes

Introduction

1. Some of the material in this section is adapted from Charles Lutz's Chapter 11, "The Search for a 'Just Security' Ethic," in *Peaceways*, Charles P. Lutz and Jerry L. Folk (Minneapolis: Augsburg, 1983). Mr. Lutz also prepared the items for group discussion which accompany each chapter of this book.
2. Quinn, Gary J., "Pacifism and the Just War: Are They Compatible?" *Dialog*, August 1972.

Chapter 1

1. One list of seven criteria, used often in American Lutheran Church documents since the Vietnam debate, is repeated in *Peaceways*, p. 146. A different set, apparently eight or nine, though not clearly numbered, is given in a Lutheran Church in America draft of 1983 on "Peace and Politics."
2. See Roland Bainton, *Christian Attitudes Toward Peace and War* (Nashville: Abingdon, 1979).

Chapter 2

1. Cf. Frederick H. Russell, *The Just War in the Middle Ages* (New York: Cambridge University Press, 1975).

Chapter 3

1. Telford Taylor, "War Crimes," pp. 425ff., and Richard Wasserstrom, "The Laws of War," pp. 455ff., in Malham M. Wakin, ed., *War, Morality, and the Military Profession* (Boulder: Westview, 1979).

Chapter 4

1. Cf. John Howard Yoder, *Nevertheless: The Varieties of Religious Pacifism* (Scottdale: Herald Press, 1971), pp. 14-18.
2. William V. O'Brien, noting that recent papal doctrines accentuate the difficulty of control or discrimination, asks why that should matter; do they mean immunity or proportion? The logical response is that control or discrimination is the precondition of respecting any or either

restraint, thereby uncontrollability becomes a vice in its own right. Even before the illegitimate use occurs, the uncontrollable instrument is illegitimate.

3. See Telford Taylor, *Nuremberg and Vietnam: An American Tragedy* (Quadrangle Books, 1970). Taylor was the U.S. Chief Counsel at the Nuremberg War Crimes Trials following World War II.

4. Martin Luther, "Whether Soldiers, Too, Can Be Saved," *Luther's Works,* vol. 46 (Philadelphia: Fortress Press, 1967), p. 130. See Appendix 2B below, p. 88.

5. A strong, relatively early statement of the negative just-war reading on Vietnam was the article by Philip Wogaman, "A Moral Reassessment of Our War in Vietnam," *Christian Century* (4 January 1967): 7.

6. See, for instance, *National Service and Selective Service Reform,* a policy statement of the American Lutheran Church's Fifth General Convention, October 1970.

Chapter 5

1. In Malham M. Wakin, *War, Morality, and the Military Profession* (Boulder: Westview, 1979), pp. 424ff., 454, 461ff.

2. Michael Walzer, *Just and Unjust Wars* (New York: Basic Books, 1977), pp. 253ff.

3. Walzer, p. 173. Most recently the scholarly debate has been reviewed by the book: *Doing Evil to Achieve Good,* edited by Richard McCormick and Paul Ramsey (Chicago: Loyola, 1978). Some would tend to argue that all of the four criteria for permissible "double-effect" decisions can be reduced to sophisticated calculations of consequential utility. Others want to see the entire doctrine as an effort, classically normal and still important today, to safeguard some notion of multiple intrinsic moral duties and limits, even in situations of complex and tragic compromises.

The skeptics who are unconvinced by the entire system point out especially that to say that one does not "intend" the evil results of one's deeds, even though one chooses so to act with the full knowledge that those results will follow criterion 1 (p. 18), is a sophistry. They say that criterion 4 is petitionary, since the entire argument is set up to explain why some things that are wrong in themselves must nevertheless be done because of complicated conflict situations. The advocates of the adequacy of the double-effect theory have not made clear how to distinguish between intrinsically wrong things which one may *never* do and other intrinsically wrong things which one may do under the above restrictions. The book-long debate does not even notice this challenge.

4. Quoted here from the 1957 original. The text is less clear in Thomas Taylor and Robert S. Bilheimer, *Christians and the Prevention of War in an Atomic Age* (London: SCM, 1961). This section is not cited in Donald Durnbaugh, *On Earth Peace* (Elgin, IL: Brethren Press, 1978), pp. 185ff., but parallel argument from the same document is provided.
5. Paul Ramsey, *War and Christian Conscience* (Durham, N.C.: Duke University Press, 1961), pp. 151-152.
6. John Courtney Murray, *Morality and Modern War* (New York: Council on Religion and International Affairs, 1959), pp. 15-16. Also in *Theological Studies*.
7. *Ibid.*
8. *Ibid.*
9. Robert W. Tucker, *The Just War: A Study in Contemporary American Doctrine* (Baltimore: Johns Hopkins, 1960), especially the chapter "The American Doctrine," pp. 11ff.
10. James F. Childress, "Just War Criteria," in *War or Peace? The Search for New Answers,* Thomas Shannon, ed. (Maryknoll, N.Y.: Orbis Books, 1980), pp. 151ff.

Chapter 6

1. See the bibliography on "Alternative Modes of National Defense."
2. I know of only one exception to the above description: the efforts of the American Lutheran Church during the past decade. The ALC, along with other U.S. Lutheran bodies, has developed study materials on the just-war tradition. In its own work with parishes and young men facing the prospect of military service, it has placed its official stance and its counsel in the setting of the tradition. Its 1982 policy statement, "Mandate for Peacemaking," rejects any use of weapons of mass destruction (nuclear, chemical, biological) on the basis of just-war criteria. It has also convened a group of its military chaplains to explore the consequences of just-war thinking for the ministry of chaplains in the nuclear age.

Appendices

Appendix 1   Martin of Tours

In the meantime, as the barbarians were rushing within the two divisions of Gaul, Julian the Apostate, bringing an army together at the city of the Vaugiones, began to distribute a donative to the soldiers. As was the custom in such a case, they were called forward, one by one, until it came to the turn of Martin. Then, indeed, judging it a suitable opportunity for seeking his discharge— for he did not think it would be proper for him, if he were not to continue in the service, to receive a donative —he said to Caesar, "Hitherto I have served you as a soldier: allow me now to become a soldier to God: let the man who is to serve thee receive thy donative: I am the soldier of Christ: it is not lawful for me to fight." Then truly the tyrant stormed on hearing such words, declaring that from fear of the battle, which was to take place on the morrow, and not from any religious feeling, Martin withdrew from the service. But Martin, full of courage, yea, all the more resolute from the danger that had been set before him exclaimed, "If this conduct of mine is ascribed to cowardice, not to faith, I will take my stand unarmed before the line of battle tomorrow, and in the name of the Lord Jesus, protected by the sign of the cross, and not by shield or helmet, I will safely penetrate the ranks of the enemy." He is ordered, therefore, to be thrust back into prison, determined on proving his words true by exposing himself unarmed to the barbarians. But, on the following day, the enemy sent ambassadors to treat about peace and surrendered both themselves and all their possessions. In these circumstances who can doubt that this victory was due to the saintly man? It was granted him that he should not be sent unarmed to the fight. And although the good Lord could have preserved his own soldier, even amid the swords and darts of the enemy, yet that his blessed eyes might not be pained by witnessing the death of others, he removed all necessity for fighting. For Christ did not require to secure any other victory in behalf of his own soldier than that, the enemy being subdued without bloodshed, no one should suffer death.

(From the *Life of St. Martin* by Sulpicius Severus)

Appendix 2   Martin Luther on the Duty of Selective Objection

A. From the *Treatise on Good Works*

But if, as often happens, the temporal power and authorities, or whatever they call themselves, would compel a subject to do something contrary to the command of God, or hinder him from doing what God commands, obedience ends and the obligation ceases. In such a case a man has to say what St. Peter said to the rulers of the Jews, "We must obey God rather than men" [Acts 5:29]. He did not say, "We must not obey men," for that would be wrong. He said, "God rather than men." [It is] as if a prince desired to go to war, and his cause was clearly unrighteous; we should neither follow nor help such a prince, because God had commanded us not to kill our neighbor or do him a wrong. Likewise, if the prince were to order us to bear false witness, steal, lie or deceive, and the like [we should refuse]. In such cases we should indeed give up our property and honor, our life and limb, so that God's commandments remain.

(From *Luther's Works,* vol. 44, p. 100)

B. From *Whether Soldiers, Too, Can Be Saved*

A second question: "Suppose my lord were wrong in going to war," I reply: If you know for sure that he is wrong, then you should fear God rather than men, Acts 4 [5:29], and you should neither fight nor serve, for you cannot have a good conscience before God. "Oh no," you say, "my lord would force me to do it; he would take away my fief and would not give me my money, pay, and wages. Besides, I would be despised and put to shame as a coward, even worse, as a man who did not keep his word and deserted his lord in need." I answer: You must take that risk and, with God's help, let whatever happens, happen. He can restore it to you a hundredfold, as he promises in the gospel, "Whoever leaves house, farm, wife, and property, will receive a hundredfold," etc. [Matt. 19:29].

(From *Luther's Works,* vol. 46, p. 130)

Questions for Discussion

Chapter 1   The Quest to Make War Moral

1. Discuss "The Simplest Criteria" outlined on p. 18. Ask the group to apply them to any war situation with which it is generally familiar, e.g., the American Revolutionary War, the Mexican War of the 1840s, World War II, the Vietnam War, the Malvinas/Falklands dispute between Argentina and Britain of 1982.

2. Do people in the group (if part of a religious community which subscribes to it) believe they have received adequate instruction in the just-war tradition? What would they suggest be done to teach it in the churches? Is it the kind of subject matter that should be taught in the public schools?

3. Does the group agree with Yoder's suggestion that national political leaders find the just-war criteria difficult to combine with the demands of the office. Think of the U.S. president's role as civilian commander-in-chief. Cite some examples of tough decisions in which the criteria would have applied.

The discussion questions on pp. 89-93 were prepared by Charles P. Lutz.

Chapter 2   Just-War Tradition in Its Medieval Context

1. We usually think of the Middle Ages as bloody and war-filled. Yet there were some significant social restraints: few could be enlisted in the actual fighting, certain areas were off-limits to combat, and specific times of the year were to be free of fighting. Contrast such arrangements with our century and its tendency toward total war. What role did the church play in inhibiting all-out war in the Middle Ages? What role does the church play today in limiting the excess of war?

2. Let the group think of examples from history of dehumanizing the enemy, that is, presenting the adversary as being something less than human and therefore having no rights. What are we to make of charges such as "the Soviet system is the focus of evil in today's world" (speech by President Ronald Reagan to National Association of Evangelicals, Orlando, Florida, March 8, 1983)? Does the biblical expectation that Christians are to "love your enemy" have any place in modern international realities?

3. If you accept the validity of a just war, do you believe that participation in such a war is nevertheless sinful? It is curious that the basic creed of Lutheranism, the Augsburg Confession, can say, "Christians may without sin . . . engage in just wars" (Article 16)—curious because Lutheran understanding of the human condition normally argues that *all* human activity is touched by sin, and all human beings stand in need of daily forgiveness. Can something be justifiable and still sinful? Or do you think an evil deed can be "without sin" if it prevents a greater evil from being done?

Chapter 3   Weakening the War Restraints

1. Yoder claims that the Protestant mainline traditions, in giving the just-war ethic creedal recognition, have

given it status beyond the realm of simply self-evident human reasoning. Roman Catholics, on the other hand, continue to view the ethic as something less than dogma (which the faithful are expected to follow). Is this why it seems easier for Roman Catholics to be sympathetic to pacifism? Can you think of other reasons why pacifism seems to have been traditionally unacceptable within such Protestant traditions as the Presbyterian and Lutheran?

2. How can we explain the fact that warfare in the name of God has loomed so large in human history? First the crusades and then, after the Reformation, a century of religious wars between Christian groups plagued Europe and the Middle East. Where in today's world are the examples of "righteous violence"? Are we forever destined to make our enemies into God's enemies? Recall that in the Old Testament God often used the national enemies of Israel to *correct* Israel. What should that suggest to Americans who like to think God is "on our side"?

3. Yoder refers to the righteous insurrection. The American Revolution was presented to the world community by our colonial leaders as a just cause, using the traditional arguments of the just-war ethic (see the Declaration of Independence). How would you apply the criteria of the just war in today's revolutionary situations? Think of Namibia, El Salvador, the Palestinians, Poland.

Chapter 4   Hopes for Limiting War

1. Ask those who have served in the military how they were taught the moral guidelines for conducting warfare. Do they feel it was done adequately? Who should be responsible for teaching it? What role, if any, does the group see for military chaplains? What should the

churches expect of their clergy who serve as chaplains, with regard to the war/peace ethic of the respective religious communities?

2. Yoder suggests that most military-age young men who conscientiously refused participation in the Vietnam War did so on the basis of just-war criteria rather than traditional pacifism. That is, they were *selective* conscientious objectors, rather than *general* (all-war) COs. Do you agree? What does the group recall about the support selective objectors received in their own religious communities?

3. Efforts in 1971 to amend the Selective Service Act to provide for selective conscientious objection were unsuccessful. Many of the just-war tradition religious groups testified in favor of legalizing SCO, but there was little support in Congress. (Senator Philip Hart of Michigan led the campaign, but in the Senate his proposal received only 12 votes.) How do you feel about making selective objection to combatant service a legal option? What would be the problems with it? What would be constructive about having such a provision? (See also Lutz's discussion in the introduction.)

Chapter 5   The Tradition and the Real World

1. How does the group feel about George Orwell's point that once war has been entered it is better to get it over with as quickly as possible, without limiting the means by which it is conducted? Should children and the elderly have any more protection than young men who happen to be drafted? Is the idea of noncombatant immunity a has-been?

2. The toughest question of all those raised by Yoder may be the one about surrender as moral obligation. Can members of the group think of circumstances in which the just-war ethic would require surrender as

the logical option? Where are the moral limits to what a nation may do in order to win?

3. Do you agree with Yoder that most Christians throughout history—and also today—are not actually in the just-war tradition, in their own personal ethics? Are most in the crusade or national-interest streams? Ask members of the group, if they are willing, to indicate which of the four ethical frameworks they feel is closest to their own position.

Chapter 6   Making the Tradition Credible

1. How can we put appropriate resources and energy into building peace? What would a nonviolent alternative to the CIA look like? Has the group heard of the proposal for establishment of a National Academy for Peace and Conflict Resolution? Legislation has been introduced in Congress to create such an institution, which would prepare leadership for resolution of conflicts by means other than military force. How does the group view such a proposal? (For more information, contact National Peace Academy Campaign, 110 Maryland Av. NE, Washington, DC 20002.)

2. Why do you think it is difficult for the organized church to show support for its members who struggle with questions of conscience around matters of war and military policies? How can the local church be helpful to its members on this point? What can national churches do that would be helpful?

3. Before concluding the group's discussion, consider developing a strategy for sharing the concerns of this study with others in your congregation. Think especially of children and youth, those of a future generation who will be inheriting our war-prone world. Check the bibliography for additional helps.

Bibliography

Just-war thinking

Bainton, Roland. *Christian Attitudes Toward War and Peace.* Nashville: Abingdon, 1979. Updated edition of the classic treatment of Christian teachings on war and peace. Indispensable historical perspective.

Durnbaugh, Donald. *On Earth Peace.* Elgin, IL: Brethren Press, 1978. A collection of documents from 20 years of ecumenical conversations between representatives of the historic Peace Churches and European Protestants.

Fortas, Abe. *Concerning Dissent and Civil Disobedience.* New York: Signet, 1970 (out of print). Includes discussion on selective conscientious objection. Former Supreme Court justice is sympathetic but finally negative to recognizing SCO in U.S. draft law.

Luther, Martin. "Temporal Authority: To What Extent It Should Be Obeyed" (1523). *Luther's Works,* vol. 45. Philadelphia: Fortress, 1962. "Treatise on Good Works" (1520). *Luther's Works,* vol. 44. Philadelphia: Fortress, 1966. "Whether Soldiers, Too, Can Be Saved" (1526). *Luther's Works,* vol. 46. Philadelphia: Fortress, 1967. Most pertinent of Luther's writings on obedience to human authority.

Lutz, Charles P.; Folk, Jerry L.; et al. *Peaceways.* Minneapolis: Augsburg, 1983. Includes chapters on application of just-war tradition and pacifism to threat of nuclear war.

Niebanck, Richard J. *Conscience, War and the Selective Objector.* New York: Board of Social Ministry, Lutheran Church in America, 1970. Applies just-war ethic to military conscription issues.

Ramsey, Paul. *The Just War: Force and Political Responsibility.* New York: Scribner's, 1968 (OP). A detailed statement of the case for the just-war ethic by a Presbyterian ethicist.

Shannon, Thomas A., ed. *War or Peace? The Search for New Answers*. Maryknoll: Orbis, 1980. A symposium.

Wakin, Malham M., ed. *War, Morality, and the Military Profession*. Boulder: Westview, 1979. A collection of earlier articles on the legality of war.

Walzer, Michael. *Just and Unjust Wars*. New York: Basic Books, 1977. The definitive contemporary philosophical text, illustrated with considerable anecdotal material.

Yoder, John Howard. *Nevertheless: The Varieties of Religious Pacifism*. Scottdale: Herald Press, 1971.

Yoder, John Howard. *What Would You Do?* Scottdale: Herald Press, 1983. Analyzes the "last resort" argument in anecdotal terms.

Alternative modes of national defense

American Friends Service Committee. *In Place of War: An Inquiry into Nonviolent National Defense*. New York: Grossman, 1962 (OP).

Boserup, Anders and Mack, Andrew. *War without Weapons: Nonviolence in National Defense*. New York: Schocken, 1975.

Boulding, Kenneth. *Conflict and Defense*. New York: Harper & Row, 1963 (OP).

Curle, Adam. *Making Peace*. London: Tavistock Publications, 1971.

King-Hall, Stephen. *Defense in a Nuclear Age*. Nyack, NY: Fellowship, 1959 (OP).

Robert, Adam, ed. *The Strategy of Civilian Defense*. London: Faber & Faber, 1970. Also Baltimore: Penguin, 1969, under the title *Civilian Resistance as National Defense*.

Sharp, Gene. *Exploring Nonviolent Alternatives*. Boston: Porter Sargent, 1970 (OP).

Sharp, Gene. *Making the Abolition of War a Realistic Goal*. New York: Institute for World Order, 1980.

Sharp, Gene. *Making Europe Unconquerable: A Civilian-Based Deterrence and Defense System*. New York: Institute for World Order, 1983.

Sharp, Gene. *The Politics of Nonviolent Action*. Boston: Porter Sargent, 1974.

Sider, Ronald and Tucker, Richard. "International Aggression and Non-Military Defense." *Christian Century* (6-13 July 1983): 643-647.

Sider, Ronald and Taylor, Richard K. *Nuclear Holocaust and Christian Hope*, Downers Grove, IL: Inter-Varsity, 1982.